WHOSE HOUSING C

Assets and home
in a changing econoiiy

Nick Gallent

P

First published in Great Britain in 2019 by

Policy Press
University of Bristol
1-9 Old Park Hill
Bristol
BS2 8BB
UK
t: +44 (0)117 954 5940
pp-info@bristol.ac.uk
www.policypress.co.uk

North America office:
Policy Press
c/o The University of Chicago Press
1427 East 60th Street
Chicago, IL 60637, USA
t: +1 773 702 7700
f: +1 773-702-9756
sales@press.uchicago.edu
www.press.uchicago.edu

© Policy Press 2019

British Library Cataloguing in Publication Data
A catalogue record for this book is available from the British Library

Library of Congress Cataloging-in-Publication Data
A catalog record for this book has been requested

978-1-4473-4531-2 hardback
978-1-4473-4607-4 paperback
978-1-4473-4606-7 ePdf
978-1-4473-4608-1 ePub
978-1-4473-4609-8 Mobi

The rights of Nick Gallent to be identified as author of this work has been asserted by him in accordance with the Copyright, Designs and Patents Act 1988.

All rights reserved: no part of this publication may be reproduced, stored in a retrieval system, or transmitted in any form or by any means, electronic, mechanical, photocopying, recording, or otherwise without the prior permission of Policy Press.

The statements and opinions contained within this publication are solely those of the editor and contributors and not of the University of Bristol or Policy Press. The University of Bristol and Policy Press disclaim responsibility for any injury to persons or property resulting from any material published in this publication.

Policy Press works to counter discrimination on grounds of gender, race, disability, age and sexuality.

Cover design by Andrew Corbett
Front cover image: Andrew Corbett

To my daughters, Marta and Elena:
You've been right all along – 'It's not fair.'

Contents

List of figures

Key terms

A small number of terms, specific to housing and planning policy development in England and the UK, are used regularly in this book. Their meaning is noted here for later reference. Acronyms are expanded within the text, and many other terms – with meanings that become clear later on – are not listed here.

Affordable housing   A type of housing (or special product) that is often delivered today as part of a planning agreement with private developers. Affordable housing, for rent or purchase (including starter homes), is included within private housing schemes.

Affordable rent   Rent discounted against the full market level. Affordable housing may now be 'affordable rent', although the level of rent is not related to local earnings.

Buy to let   Buying homes to let to others. Also refers to *buy-to-let* mortgage products.

Community land trust   A social-purpose trust established by a community group to hold land on which community infrastructure, including affordable homes, might be built.

Help to buy   Government support for first-time buyers in the form of interest-free/low-interest loans designed to aid these buyers' entry into the housing market.

Imputed rent   An estimate of the monetary value of housing services consumed by households who are not actually renting their homes, equivalent to the rent they would otherwise pay, were they renting.

Land rent   Rent paid directly to an owner of land, or ground rent paid to a superior landlord by a lessee.

Residential mortgage-backed securities   A tradeable financial product backed by the income derived from residential mortgages.

Right to buy   The right given to local authority secure tenants, after 1980, to buy their homes with a discount.

Social rent   A nominal rent, usually set well below the market level.

Stamp duty   A progressive tax levied on property transactions – paid by a house purchaser.

Starter homes   Refers to government's recent scheme to include 'starter homes' in market developments, available to purchase at a 20% discount.

Acknowledgements

This is a very sustainable book – parts of it have been recycled from previous publications. Chapter 1 has paragraphs that have been adapted from a 2017 critical commentary for *Urban Studies* and a contribution to *Planning Practice: Critical Perspectives from the UK* (Routledge, 2018). Likewise, Chapters 3 and 6 have some cannibalised ideas from prior contributions to the *Journal of Urban Regeneration and Renewal* (2016) and *Town Planning Review* (2018). But for the most part, the book comprises new material and commentary, interwoven with data, tables and graphs adapted from other sources – all of which are of course cited.

I am grateful to my recent co-authors – Dan Durrant, Neil May and Phoebe Stirling, all at the Bartlett UCL – for their immense input into our collaborative ventures, and also to the UCL Grand Challenges team, James Paskins and Ian Scott, for supporting our 'rethinking housing' initiative. I would also like to thank colleagues who have read and commented on different parts of this book and for pointing out the glaring errors and omissions – and plain silliness – that I have since attempted to correct. Particular thanks go to John Tomaney, John Parr and the anonymous reviewer engaged by Policy Press. I am conscious, however, of not having been able to respond to all comments and suggestions – and that the book remains a partial and imperfect account of a hugely complex area of scholarly enquiry, public policy and social experience.

The work of other colleagues and co-authors at UCL, and elsewhere, has also been important over the years in shaping my broader thinking on housing and development debates. These include Mark Tewdwr-Jones, Matthew Carmona, Claudio de Magalhaes, Daniela Ciaffi, Iqbal Hamiduddin, Mark Scott, Menelaos Gkartzios, Mark Bevan, Madhu Satsangi, Dave Shaw, Sue Kidd, Marco Bianconi, Johan Andersson, Cecilia Wong, Rhys Jones, Gwyn Williams, Bill Edwards, Chris Allen, Ed Shepherd, Nicole Gurran, Rebecca Chiu, Sonia Freire Trigo, Meri Juntti and many others. If I haven't named you here, I'm profusely sorry and will buy you a drink soon.

At Policy Press, Emily Watt encouraged me to write this book. In fact, *she made me do it*. And while Emily was on maternity leave, Sarah Bird, Sarah Connolly, Laura Cope, Jamie Askew and Leonie Drake kept the project on track. I would also like to thank Sandra Mather at the University of Liverpool. Over the last decade, she has redrawn most of the diagrams and maps that have appeared in my books and articles – and everything in this one.

The most important acknowledgement always comes last: to my family, my wife Manuela Madeddu and daughters Marta and Elena, who've tolerated my semi-constant writing in recent years, and the occasional (my wife says *regular*) accompanying tantrums.

Preface

This is another book about 'the housing crisis': housing in many parts of the UK has become expensive to rent and nearly impossible to buy for households on low, average and even good incomes. This has a range of consequences which are discussed later on. In this preface, I want to do three things. First, explain the book's title and focus; second, outline the basic argument; and third, say something about how the book is structured and why.

Besides taking inspiration from Ray Pahl's *Whose City?* (1975) and its crisp analysis of residential property classes, the title of this book – *Whose Housing Crisis?* – is a provocation, which alludes to a crisis broadly shared, and from which no one can ultimately escape, rather than a predicament affecting only those on society's economic fringe. There is a popular notion that bad housing and inequitable housing outcomes affect only a narrow section of society. But this is not so. The housing stresses faced in England and some other parts of the UK today evidence an unsustainable divide between property classes and *an endemic reliance on housing wealth to drive the national economy*. The housing crisis is pervasive; it affects everyone sooner or later, either directly in terms of personal housing circumstances or indirectly as growth built on value extraction from fixed assets stalls – and economies fail. While the economy's increased reliance on housing wealth is examined in Chapter 3, the book's titular question is most directly addressed in Chapter 5.

That chapter does not list, in any detail, the groups most or least affected by housing inequalities. There is no focus on winners or losers or on places enduring the greatest stress: market 'hotspots', gentrifying urban neighbourhoods or 'left-behind places'. Rather, I argue – at a structural level – that the housing crisis is *hardwired* into economic processes; that reliance on an unequal distribution of wealth (between rentiers and renters, and between those who create and control debt and those who endure it) to drive economies presents deep socioeconomic risks; and that the housing crisis therefore belongs to everyone dependent on this economy for their future wellbeing.

The claim that *the crisis is everyone's* (which is the answer offered to my own question – and apologies for the lack of a spoiler alert) will not satisfy all readers, many of whom will understandably wish to read structural failings in the lived experience of homelessness or the inability to access a decent home. They might argue that the crisis needs to be exposed and understood through those experiences. My answer to those readers is that a great many books have engaged in deep ethnography and drawn attention to the hardships and stresses that bad housing generates. The purpose of this book, however, is to illustrate how housing outcomes, ostensibly good or bad for different groups, always reveal deeper economic challenges and attendant consequences. These include rising inequality, declining social cohesion and a retreat from shared prosperity – consequences that provide the focus of Chapter 5. Housing is implicated in all of these challenges, and the predicament in which we now find ourselves – of escalating costs and reduced housing access – should be seen as the existential crisis of our time and not merely an outcome belonging to society's worst-off. Analyses of worst cases (and places) invariably justify 'targeted measures' that miss the structural challenges that I seek to expose in this book. There is good reason, therefore, to pose the question 'Whose housing crisis?' if the answer given – *that it is everyone's* – prompts wider interest in engineering a more equitable and sustainable housing system.

So what basic argument will I offer in this book? There are two related things that I am not going to say. I'm not going to say, firstly, that there is no housing supply (new build) challenge or, secondly, that a simple redistribution of available homes would put pay to any talk of a crisis. We know that the population is growing and that households continue to form. There are not enough new homes to meet future needs in the long term. At the same time, we also know that housing wealth is concentrated in fewer hands every year. Those with the resources are investing in housing and consuming it in ever greater quantities. Some of it is even left empty and held as pure asset. But I do not believe in any quick fix: no sudden revolution that brings a forced redistribution and kicks out the foreign buyers. In fact, the crisis is home-grown and rooted in a relationship with housing that has been created and nurtured here in the UK. There are no foreign villains in this tragedy. The argument developed is that our relationship with housing has been transformed in the latter half of the twentieth century and into the twenty-first. By 'our relationship' I mean us as individuals and the economy which sustains us. Housing is no longer primarily a social or communal good. It meets a basic need but this function has been relegated behind its role in personal finances (as investment, releasable equity and pension pot) and its related role in supporting the financial services sector and sustaining economic growth, both through the consumer confidence instilled in those fortunate enough to own their homes and the investment opportunities offered to a global market. The UK's economic growth in the early years of this century relies on us selling the family silver – land, housing, and other forms of property. But the situation is worse than that: the asset being sold isn't silver, or some other non-essential luxury good, but something far more valuable and crucial to the wellbeing, happiness and life chances of the entire population. Everyone needs to be well housed: good housing delivers not only shelter but security, opportunity, social and psychological wellbeing and the chance of good health into later life. That a relationship with housing as an 'economic good' has been allowed to dominate, to the detriment of all, is nothing short of scandalous. Keeping this central argument in sight, I will track along the pathways into this crisis – and some of the possible roads out of it – over the next six chapters.

Finally, how is the book structured? As well as being inspired by Ray Pahl, I have always found Rittel and Webber's (1973) explanation of 'wicked problems' to be extremely helpful when thinking about housing. The housing crisis is certainly 'tricky like a leprechaun' but, more than that, it evidences deeper challenges. It expresses a more pervasive economic crisis with complex roots, and which underpins and drives our changed relationship with housing. For that reason, I not only present the housing crisis as a wicked problem in general terms but use three of Rittel and Webber's characteristics of a genuinely wicked problem to structure this analysis: that 'every wicked problem can be considered to be a symptom of another problem' (p. 165); that the 'existence of ... a wicked problem can be explained in numerous ways' (p. 166) (and that the 'choice of explanation determines the nature of the problem's resolution'); and that 'solutions to wicked problems are not true or false, but good or bad' (p. 162). One of the benefits of this perspective is that it draws out the underlying and constant causes of housing stress in the UK, which is particularly acute in London and much of the southeast of England. Those who reject the idea of a housing crisis will claim that prices spike and prices fall – at different points in the market cycle, or in different places – and that periods of escalating costs will always be followed by periods of normality. But 'normality' in the UK means housing costs and access being determined not by earnings but by an underlying economic reliance on housing that ebbs and flows but never disappears. The asset relationship with housing has brought fundamental social injustice. The question of whether that relationship can be shifted – and assets transformed back into homes – is the final destination for this book.

Nick Gallent, July 2018

1

The housing crisis

England is in the grip of a housing crisis marked by rising property prices, declining affordability (relative to workplace earnings), falling rates of homeownership and rising levels of long-term renting, homelessness and general housing inequality. London, where demand for residential property outstrips market supply and where price increases have been steepest, is undoubtedly the focus of this crisis. The purpose of this book is to examine the causes of this situation, and to explore the ways in which the mixed function of housing – as *home* and *asset* – shapes patterns of consumption, housing costs, and levels of affordability and general access. It does not reject the need, in many parts of England and across the UK, to build more homes. Housing supply, however, comprises not only new dwellings added to the total housing stock; rather, supply is a composite of new and second-hand housing. Therefore, in order to understand the factors shaping affordability and access – to *all* housing – it is necessary to examine both impediments to new build (including planning as an expression of local politics and attitudes towards development) and the reasons why housing across much of the market has become increasingly expensive, with prices decoupling from earnings in many areas and becoming increasingly unaffordable.

Housing affordability – a term often used but seldom clearly defined – expresses an important relationship between household earnings and housing costs (including associated travel costs if there is a dislocation between where a household resides and where its occupants need to work). Analytical, political and practical uses of the term have been reviewed in an article by Hulchanski (1995), which remains – in my view – one of the most important contributions to understanding the concept of affordability and the attendant politics surrounding its use. When housing is said to be *affordable*, the inference is that costs – to rent or buy – are reasonable relative to household earnings. What *reasonable* means is a political call: but it needs to be expressed as a proportion of net monthly earnings for rent and a multiple of yearly gross earnings for mortgage borrowing.

Figures from the Office for National Statistics (ONS) reveal that, in the 10 years between 2007 and 2017, the ratio (or multiple) of median house price to median gross annual workplace earnings in England rose from 7.15 to 7.91 (ONS, 2018a). The rise in London over the same period was from 7.94 to 12.36. In Kensington and Chelsea, the same ratio was 40.7 in 2017. During that decade, the number of households which were 'owner-occupiers' in England fell by 31,000; the percentage of all English households owning their homes dropped from almost 68% in 2007 to just under 63% 10 years later. This fall in homeownership was mirrored by a sharp rise in private renting: from 14% to 20%. The English Housing Survey (MHCLG, 2018a) further shows that the decline in homeownership has been particularly pronounced among those aged 35 to 44: the rate among that group was 72% in 2006/07, falling to 52% 10 years later. The rate of *overcrowding* in private rented housing has remained constant, at about 5%. But the rate of *under-occupancy* in owner-occupied housing has climbed, from 39% to 51%. The term 'generation rent' is regularly used as shorthand to describe the situation revealed in the above statistics: an increasing proportion of young people, many of whom aspire to buy their own homes, are unable to do so because of increasing costs relative to stagnating earnings. At the same time, owner-occupiers have aged, paid off their mortgages (MHCLG, 2018a: 1) and now consume more housing space than they need.

The purpose of this first chapter is to introduce the housing crisis in England,[1] to consider its possible causes and its visible consequences, and also to introduce and sketch out some of the key arguments developed in later chapters. The starting point for this book is that the national appetite to consume more housing is not only driven by rising workplace earnings (for some households), but by the perceived and real function of housing – and other fixed assets – beyond utility. *Whose Housing Crisis?* is therefore concerned with housing as asset – *an economic resource* – and with its role in personal and national finances – versus housing's function as home. Its engagement with the planning system's role in promoting or discouraging new supply is relatively light, as this issue has been dealt with comprehensively elsewhere and new supply, potentially constrained by planning decisions, comprises less than 1% of total housing stock (and less than 15% of

---

[1] While the UK provides the broader economic, political and institutional context, the brunt of the housing crisis examined in this book is felt in England. The crisis of housing cost, affordability and access has key pressure points, which include London and the southeast of England, but which are also present in other urban centres across the UK and in rural areas where the processes described in this book have caused a decoupling of housing costs from workplace earnings.

sale transactions) in a typical year (see RTPI, 2007). Planning is not presented as the central driver of the housing crisis. Likewise, it is not primarily concerned with financialisation (preceded by a credit switch into fixed assets) but rather with economies' and individuals' broader relationship with housing.

The remainder of this chapter tracks through and introduces ideas expanded upon in the rest of this book. It is divided into six parts, beginning with some introductory remarks on recent (and not-so-recent) attempts to 'reframe' our understanding of housing crises, or crises of housing consumption. I then provide a preliminary view of the housing supply debate in England, marking out a territory which is explored again in Chapter 3 and returned to in Chapter 6. This focus on supply is followed by a short review of the planning system's role in facilitating, or failing to facilitate, housing delivery – completing my opening treatment of the *housing/planning nexus*. Three final introductions address the broader scope of this book, the housing crisis facing people in England (beyond the statistics) and the arrangement of the next five chapters.

Reframing the housing crisis

There have been several recent attempts to reframe housing challenges away from the housing/planning nexus. Barker (2014) has called for a response to observed housing stresses that combines actions rooted in planning with a range of fiscal measures aimed at accelerating supply while changing patterns of housing consumption. Bowie (2017) sets himself very similar goals, while Edwards (2015) places land, land rent and the economic function of housing at the heart of his analysis. Ryan-Collins et al (2017) have presented capital investment in land, 'residential capitalism', and credit supply from deregulated banks as core to the trajectory of house prices, causing a slow erosion of the link between those prices and workplace earnings, which accelerated in the early years of this century.

These and other studies have drawn attention to consumption pressures on land and housing, noting the movement of investment capital into land and property and viewing the housing crisis, to a greater or lesser degree, as a crisis of wealth, poverty and inequality rooted in the control and extraction of wealth through land rent. That crisis has been magnified by the search, by investors and financial service providers, for *new ways* to extract financial income from credit/ debt. This *financialisation* – long in the making but only recently discovered by many social scientists – has increased and broadened the asset appeal of housing, bringing land and housing debt into the domain of pension funds and other investment vehicles. Aalbers (2015, 2016), Christophers (2010), Gotham (2006, 2009) (and others) have recently been at the forefront of tracking these developments and in presenting financialisation (of housing and other fixed assets and infrastructure) as part of a new political economy that frames important questions around inequality, wealth and prosperity. This framing is relatively high-level – financialisation makes otherwise illiquid assets liquid, thereby overcoming spatial fixity and drawing global investors into property-related investment – but is core to my own analysis of housing's economic context, presented in Chapter 3. That analysis begins with the work of David Harvey.

In 1978, Harvey drew attention to the over-accumulation, and movement away, of capital from its primary (*productive*) circuit. Capital flows in three circuits: in support of the production process, in fixed capital items (forming a 'consumption fund' that includes 'built environment for production') and in a tertiary circuit encompassing research and development (R&D) and education, among other things. The built environment component of the secondary circuit serves 'jointly for both production and consumption', in that 'investment in the built environment ... entails the creation of a whole physical landscape for purposes of production, exchange and consumption' (Harvey, 1978: 106). Harvey observes that over-accumulation in the primary circuit ('too much capital produced in aggregate relative to the opportunities to employ that capital') causes a number of issues for capitalists/investors: overproduction, market glut, falling profits and surplus capital manifest in idle productive capacity and/or 'money capital lacking opportunities for profitable employment' (p. 106). This is Harvey's 'preliminary framework for the analysis of capitalist crises'.

Critically, Harvey argued that the secondary circuit – encompassing the built environment – can provide a temporary destination for the surplus capital arising from over-accumulation. Movement between these circuits is, however, constrained by capacity to achieve a ready flow of capital between the primary and secondary circuits. That flow needs to be facilitated by a 'functioning capital market', by consumer credit and mortgages and other financial instruments that 'mediate' the relations between the primary and secondary circuits. The claim here is that crises in capitalism have tended, in the past, to lead to a flow of capital into the built environment, including housing, in response to falling investment returns elsewhere. The maturation of capital markets and the creation of new financial instruments (part of the financialisation process of the late twentieth century) has resulted in the required *new ways* to mediate the relationship between circuits, meaning that the 'temporary' role of the secondary circuit in capital accumulation/profit-taking has acquired a new permanence. Housing has become part of a productive infrastructure for capital and is no longer merely part of its consumption fund.

These are *global* processes – or housing's metanarrative. Gamble (2014: 29) calls for greater attention to the 'human wills and purposes' (including of market actors) that have seen *national* frameworks align with this condition of late capitalism. Formulations of England's housing crisis are detailed later on but, by way of introduction, some national-level shifts that have transformed the function of housing and which provide tacit evidence of deeper undercurrents are noted here.

In England, housing has been transformed (in economic discourse and thereafter in the political perspective) from basic shelter, through being a gateway to social and economic opportunity (by virtue of proximity to jobs, schools and services – and also because of its centrality to a range of related activities, centred on construction and commodity production for domestic consumption), to its final manifestation as a store of wealth, investment and income for individuals and upwards to national economies. Personal investment in housing is motivated by the long climb in prices observed in many countries, with housing viewed as a reliable 'store of wealth' (Fernandez et al, 2016: 2446), able to deliver capital appreciation and rental income as added benefits. *Personal* direct investment, however, is only one component of the broader capital switch into property, which, over at least the last fifty years, has been manifest in the absorption of surplus *global* capital (accumulated and held by a mix of institutional and private investors) into fixed assets, aided by a deregulation (and maturation) of financial markets.

The way in which the UK economy has transformed, partly as a result of this capital switch, and the implications of that transformation for the trajectory of house prices and public (tax) revenues is explored later in this book. A second major shift – which was a necessary prerequisite and outcome of the first – is the withdrawal of the state from housing production and management, leaving a situation in which 'the market' *has to* 'step in' and meet a broad mix of needs, demands and aspirations, and in which deregulated financial markets *can* exploit the investment potential of fixed assets, including housing, and drive an 'urbanisation of capital' (Harvey, 1978, 1985).

The will of the market, and market actors, has become more dominant since the Second World War. State intervention has been rolled back and it is the market function and exchange value of housing that has come into ascendency – turning housing into a wealth machine for some, but a poverty machine for others – generating gross inequalities for those locked out of the financial benefits of homeownership (Edwards, 2002; Rolnik, 2013). These big changes are examined later on, but they must contend with the popular view that supplying more homes is the answer to the housing crisis. This view has validity, especially if the housing crisis is viewed not only as a crisis for people but also capital (that is, the crisis of affordability reveals the tension caused by housing's function as an investment destination, but that same crisis locks investors out of the market and disrupts the switch of new capital into the built environment). Supplying more *homes* is important for people, but supplying more *assets* expands the consumption fund – providing a place to park, exchange and grow wealth – and helps stave off potential crises of capitalist production. Western prosperity depends on opening up new land to development and realising its value, through the extraction of rent, by building homes on it.

Putting this metanarrative to one side for the moment, and returning to the popular supply debate, how does the supply of more homes relate to the housing crisis affecting people – experienced by households needing homes and characterised by rising housing costs relative to earnings? And what culpability does planning have for the outcomes quantified at the beginning, and qualified at the end, of this chapter?

Supplying new homes

How housing affordability and inequality challenges impact on people is introduced towards the end of this chapter, but then expanded upon in Chapter 5. The pressing concern of this book is to expose the cause of these challenges so that remedies, interim and more fundamental, might be identified. The obvious solution to a generalised housing problem is to supply more new housing through a combination of market and non-market providers. Growing housing supply will result in a shrinking of the housing problem. But what is housing supply? In the current debate in England, housing supply is generally taken to mean *new housing*, mainly delivered by private enterprise (especially volume producers) but also by some local authorities, housing associations and self-builders. The supply of housing in any market, however, is a composite of existing housing for rent or purchase plus anything newly built becoming available. Supply is the economists' expression for the amount of housing 'coming onto the market', new and old, for those who need or desire it. But because that current debate focuses on *new housing*, analysis of 'supply constraint' (said to be responsible for declining affordability relative to earnings and inequalities between wealthier or poorer buyers) focuses on a mix of politics and planning (and associated regulation).

There is no doubt that politics and planning can and do act to constrain the supply of new housing (that is, new build and conversion/subdivision). Housing development occurs in a political space and is hence contested. Second-hand housing is, however, a large part of the supply composite. Patterns of consumption in that part of the market (alongside patterns of consumption in the new-build component) will impact on supply if housing provides not only home but also a place to park money (to 'splash cash') and is consumed for reasons ranging from status competition to expected revenue yield or capital return. The parking of money by investors (which takes many forms – see above and Chapter 4) constrains the supply of housing across all segments of the market, impacting on prices and therefore on affordability and access. As the second-hand market becomes increasingly inaccessible in many places, analysis of the housing problem splits along two paths. One path focuses on the investment challenge and the other on the need to supply more new homes. The investment, or *disruptive consumption*, thesis quickly identifies its chief villains: overseas buyers (Rossall Valentine, 2015) and those seeking second homes (Paris, 2010). The new supply advocates direct their criticism at politicians and planners, who have failed to facilitate the delivery of enough new homes, either because of their lack of investment in infrastructure or because, as regulators, they stand in the way of *the market* – an entity viewed as discrete from regulatory influence. Regulation, it is claimed, is a potential source of uncertainty and risk to investment in housebuilding (see de Magalhaes et al, 2018).

The reality is that not enough homes are being built *and* those homes that have been built, in the past, have been refunctioned. The housing crisis is rooted in both inadequate supply and disruptive consumption, with both of these causes anchored in the changed relationship with housing introduced in the last section. The politics of new build, and local resistance to it, is – in part – due to the transformation of housing into an asset and the consequent defence of property values (see, for example, Coelho et al, 2017). Disruptive consumption, in turn, is motivated by the desire to hold housing as asset for a variety of reasons that I hope to make clear in later chapters. These two forces come together to create a much broader housing supply problem than one focused solely on new build. Housing supply may well be adequate – or could be made adequate across the new-build and second-hand markets – relative to the number of families forming and needing a home (flagged in periodic projections of household formation and discussed in greater detail below). But it is, and will remain, inadequate relative to the amount of wealth and credit (together forming a 'surplus capital') flowing into housing from a variety of national and international sources. Moreover, more *homes* are needed for people to live in and, as the economy is dependent on the capital and tax revenues extracted from the 'physical landscape' of the built environment, more *built assets* are needed to drive the economy, or rather to sustain the crucial relationship between Harvey's primary and secondary circuits.

Before extending this composite view of the housing crisis later in this chapter and elsewhere in this book, it would perhaps be useful to provide a sketch of the planning system's recent engagements with the housing market and housebuilding industry. Much later in this book, I will examine the role that planning might play in supplying more new homes and easing the impacts of consumption pressure across the entire housing market.

Planning and the 'market' for housing

Planning policy and practice in relation to housing (and the broader 'politics' of new build) seems always to be in the dock, accused of clumsy attempts to direct the market and ending up impeding the supply of new homes, thereby pushing up prices and restricting access. Planning is seen by its critics as a market inhibitor, creating uncertainty for the development industry (de Magalhaes et al, 2018) and occupying centre stage in the housing crisis. Again, this world view supposes that the crisis is one generated largely by low levels of new housing supply, with that supply diminished by land-use policy (including urban containment policies such as green belt) and local planning practice. It was noted above that supply is more than just new build, but rather the composite availability of homes, new and old, coming onto the market at any one time. Similarly, the supply perspective seems to offer a strangely local and closed view of the demands on that supply (that is, newly built housing and second-hand properties being offered to the market). Either that, or it supposes that additions to the total housing stock can satiate a composite demand for housing that comprises the 'requirement' arising from new household formation and households migrating permanently to the UK for work or other reasons, households trading up (or down) through the market as their needs change, households trading up through the market for reasons of investment, domestic buyers seeking investment properties (including *buy to let*) or second homes, overseas buyers (not domiciled in the UK) acquiring residential property for its capital appreciation potential, and institutional investors acquiring permissioned land and residential buildings for the purpose of creating asset-backed portfolio funds.

The total composite demand for housing has the potential to far exceed the requirement arising from demographic change. Over the last five years or so, the projection of newly arising demand (in England) has been fairly stable: around 240,000 households forming and needing homes each year. This is then taken to be the *annualised target* for housing completions, which exceeded 160,000 in England in 2017/18, and almost 190,000 across the UK (MHCLG Live Table 209).[2] Planning should be 'facilitating' this level of new supply: by allocating land for housing in the right places and speedily granting development permission, attaching as few conditions on development as possible and creating as much certainty as possible for private enterprise. Nationally, the planning system is viewed as a hindrance to this level of delivery because it insists on constraining supply where 'demand' is thought to be greatest – in and around London – through its green belt policy (Mace et al, 2016). Locally, the sorts of big schemes needed if supply is to be increased seem forever mired in local conflict and uncertainty and often fail to get off the ground (Gurran et al, 2016), at least not on the scale that was originally envisaged.

Local planning authorities are accused of having too much power and too little interest in seeing development succeed (Barker, 2004). The response has been sustained criticism of green belt policy and planning more generally as the major cause of the housing crisis (Hilber, 2015). Considerable attention, and critique, has been devoted to the way local planning allocates land for new housing and then mediates the development process, requiring that proposed housing schemes meet various public tests ahead of final permission. The practice of planning for housing is not solely concerned with allocating land for new development. But the way in which planning, and local planning practice, facilitates or impedes land supply has long been the primary concern of national policy. Therefore, a single question is addressed here: how is land for housing allocated and how has that process sought to connect with the complexities of the market in

---

[2] MHCLG maintains live tables on key housing statistics. These figures are from Live Table 209, which can be accessed on-line. The root for these tables is: https://www. gov.uk/government/statistical-data-sets.

pursuit of welfare optimisation – a good fit between the profiles of demand and supply?

The allocation of land for housing is a key purpose of development planning practice. That purpose was set out and restated in primary legislation throughout the twentieth and into the twenty-first century. Practical advice to local authorities on how they might achieve that purpose, procedurally, was provided by the Department of the Environment in 1984 (DoE, 1984), building on earlier instructions to maintain a five-year land supply and work with the building industry on housing land availability studies (DoE, 1980). Authorities were tasked with maintaining a 'sufficient' supply of land for new housing, to be formally allocated within local plans. Four years later that same advice was rolled into new 'planning policy guidance' on housing (PPG3), and a few years after that, in 1992, a broader view of what planning should seek to achieve through its regulation of housing development was set out in a revision of that guidance. Negotiation for the inclusion of *affordable housing* in private schemes joined a shopping list of planning functions: to seek and support design quality, achieve housing mix and type, set appropriate parking standards, and strike a balance between land recycling and the use of greenfield sites through appropriate allocations.

But throughout the 1980s and into the 1990s, maintaining an 'effective' or sufficient five-year supply became a key point of contention. Despite the involvement of housebuilders in the land availability studies preceding allocations, those allocations seldom met the aspirations of private enterprise. Local practice therefore entered a period of 'planning by appeal', in which local authorities unable to demonstrate effective supply regularly saw their decisions overturned by successive secretaries of state (Adams, 2011: 954). The narrative from this point was one of strengthening the status of plans in decision-making and the replacement of Housing Availability Studies with a series of alternative tools for selecting and allocating sites for development. Urban Capacity Studies (set out in the revision of PPG3 in 2000) sought to deliver more housing on brownfield land and were introduced in tandem with a 'sequential approach' to land allocations, enabling authorities to resist development on 'green-fields' until all previously developed sites were exhausted. Adams (2011: 954–6) provides a detailed account of this transition as well as the switch back to Housing Land Availability Studies – in the form of Strategic Housing Land Availability Assessments (SHLAAs) – which were redesigned to deliver closer collaboration between local planning and the development industry. The SHLAAs were part of a new planning approach that would be more alive to market conditions and signals, largely because of the input provided by Strategic Housing Market Assessments (SHMAs), which 'were intended to provide local authorities with the necessary market data and information for decision making' (Adams, 2011: 955).

Development planning's 'clumsy' attempts to connect with market information, and the economic impacts of the planning system, have figured prominently in academic debate for several decades (from Bramley, 1993, to Hilber, 2015). Planning by appeal in the 1980s is often presented as the eruption of an inherent friction between regulation and enterprise that can be papered over – as it was in 1991, when an attempt was made to reassert the primary of local plans in decision making – but is always manifest in risks to investors, costs to developers and the undersupply of new homes. Planning practice has moved on since the 1990s and now focuses on finding and allocating 'deliverable' (viable) sites (MHCLG, 2018b), keeping allocations under regular review.

The transition from sufficiency of allocations to deliverability of development, based on more sophisticated market intelligence, can be traced back 25 years, but the impetus to transform local planning practice came from the 2004 Barker Review of Housing Supply. Barker presented existing practice as unresponsive to market change. She claimed that, for reasons of local politics (popular resistance to specific land releases justifying political rejection), allocations were not always sufficient (and effective) and sites allocated not deliverable within the timeframes envisaged. Authorities needed greater incentive to proactively pursue (and promote the case for) development with partners, and therefore contribute to meeting national housing targets (making the right allocations and actual delivery should be rewarded, according to Barker). And finally, large strategic allocations – in the form of new settlements and urban extensions – were likely to be the right responses to market signals in some places. The Barker Review was instrumental in linking housing growth to affordability and set in train a number of key shifts including:

> commissioning and publishing a controversial affordability model and establishing the controversial National Housing and Planning Advice Unit, which in 2008 produced a much-disputed target range for future housing growth in each English region. Significantly, both were predicated on macro-economic modelling, which sought to link house prices, earnings, migration patterns, household formation

and employment to land release at the regional level. This
reflected the increasing role of economics in driving spatial
policy, to the extent that the Department for Communities
and Local Government had begun to think of itself as an
'economics department'. (Adams, 2011: 957)

A subsequent Planning Policy Statement on Housing (PPS3), published
in 2006, required local planning to take market information into
account when identifying land for development and managing supply.
How this should be done was not immediately apparent. But a later
Housing Market Information Advice Note issued by DCLG made it
clear that simple demand indicators (for example, price spikes) were
inadequate to the task and allocations should be guided by Strategic
Housing Market Assessments undertaken at a sub-regional level.

This became the *affordability-led approach* to planning for housing,
predicated on the view that regional, and therefore national, housing
affordability is achievable through market-responsive planning practice
and higher rates of housebuilding. The approach supposes that increases
in workplace earnings – of new and existing resident households
– drives housing demand and therefore house prices (see earlier
discussion). More recent analyses – those that have sought a reframing
of the housing crisis – have queried the extent to which essentially *local
trends* – in demography and earnings – are able to explain patterns of
demand and price setting. The metanarrative detailed earlier in this
chapter – of a capital switch – sees capital accumulation in housing
impacting on demand either directly (through the consumption of
new housing) or indirectly (through the consumption of existing
housing and by pushing 'local demand' to the new-build segment).
Conventional models, including those constructed in the 2000s for
government, match earnings and household formation to required
building rates but assume that, by and large, housing functions as home.
Models that acknowledge the asset function of housing – and factor in
the attractiveness of residential property to investors – point to a level
of demand far in excess of household formation rates underpinned
by workplace earnings.

The task for the planning system and local planning practice, if
responses to the housing crisis are all to be on the supply side, is to get
to grips with a much broader array of market evidence (that quantifies
new patterns of housing function, use and consumption) and then help
achieve a step change in housing supply through a much faster, flexible
(yet certain), streamlined and incentivised development planning
process. But, of course, many will doubt whether this increase in

supply is desirable or achievable, or whether residential property should be viewed, in the main, as an economic infrastructure: a commodity sold in the global marketplace to sustain economic growth.

Moreover, analyses of the wider political economy of the crisis, some of which have been introduced earlier, suggest that it is not all down to a troublesome planning process, but driven by new patterns of consumption. Reflecting again on the 240,000 figure quoted above, it seems simplistic that this should be taken as an annual building target. Others (including Cheshire et al, 2014) have long argued that economics (and earnings) should be the starting point for understanding the demand for housing (and its price – see Meen, 2011) and the level of housebuilding (or composite supply) needed to meet that demand. Economic drivers need to figure prominently in demand projections. This point is emphasised by Whitehead (2016: 419), who shows that stability in real house prices in England will be delivered only when new annual supply of 400,000 homes is achieved and sustained. At that point, workplace earnings and house prices will rise at the same rate. But that does not mean that housing will become more affordable, as the ratios between earnings and property prices are already extremely stretched in some places, especially in and around London. To achieve increased affordability – that is, to close the gap between median (and lower quartile) earnings and prices – the sustained rate of building will need to greatly exceed 400,000 homes each year. In light of recent and historic building rates (detailed in Chapter 4), achieving this figure through new development alone seems unlikely, although local authorities might make a bigger contribution in the future by operating through local housing companies (Hackett, 2017; Morphet and Clifford, 2017). But if the required build rate is far greater than assessments of need, then two obvious questions arise: what is driving this demand for housing in England and what is housing really for?

Beyond the English housing/planning nexus

In the next five chapters, I will venture beyond the housing/planning nexus, briefly introduced in the last two sections. A range of reasons for current housing outcomes are explored – pathways that have led to these outcomes and which, in some instances, are complicit in the repurposing of housing in England.

Chapter 4 looks at how postwar public housing programmes have been reined back since the 1970s. Housing has become a *private matter*, both in terms of how it is produced (by either a contract or speculative housing industry) and how it is consumed (by individual purchasers, with cash or credit). The process of privatisation – and commodification of housing as exchange good – paved the way for a refunctioning of housing as asset, and coincided (in Western Europe, North America and Australasia) with a weakening manufacturing base and a new reliance on profit-taking from fixed assets as a mainstay of post- or late-industrial economies (Edwards, 2002, 2015). In short, housing gained a broader economic function in the late twentieth century, and this is analysed in Chapter 3. Demand in excess of need and supply, and therefore upward pressure on house prices, boosts consumer confidence, drives consumption across the economy, and helps sustain tax revenues in support of the state (directly in the form of property transaction and consumption taxes and indirectly through taxes on other forms of consumption). The collateral qualities of housing have underpinned investor demand, with that demand often supported by less restrictive bank lending practices and by the reregulation of lending and the creation of 'new money' in support of housing consumption. These two drivers – investment and credit, which have reshaped the housing market – are examined at length in Chapters 3 and 4, and briefly introduced here.

In the years following the 2008 global financial crisis (GFC), there has been greater concern among analysts for the impact of credit availability on housing consumption and house prices. More attention has been given to the channels by which credit affects price (Duca et al, 2010) and how easier access to loans (as banks prioritise lending on real estate) resulted, in the years leading up to the crisis, in a pattern of 'overinvestment' (initially in the US subprime market) that raised personal debt to the point where it was unsustainable and banks were unable to retrieve the cost of 'bad loans' from default, foreclosure and onward sale. Housing had become overvalued (see Keen, 2018) to the point where the value of the fixed asset bore diminishing relationship to the size of the debt attached to it. The results are well known: this level of overinvestment had global implications and underscored the vulnerability of banks and national economies which 'implicitly treat housing markets as liquid and efficient' (Duca et al, 2010: 204).

More specifically, lending preferences and practices decoupled the value of property from workplace earnings. The banking sector in the UK more than doubled the supply of money to the property market and financial sector in the run-up to the GFC, causing an escalation of demand for high-quality collateral assets and drawing in new speculators. A self-reinforcing inflationary process set in, with the increase in demand for such assets further driving up their price, which in turn generated an upward spiral of borrowing and price inflation.

The behaviour of banks has been critical in skewing the economy towards housing dependency and away from business or manufacturing growth. If a business fails then money lent by a bank to support it is lost. If, on the other hand, a homebuyer defaults on a mortgage, the bank recovers and sells on the property in a market where prices are set by the credit liberalisation of which it is a part. The bank may profit from the default, enjoying the equity growth now lost to the former mortgagee. But in order to avoid this situation becoming a norm, or just too regular an occurrence, interest rates are set to make loans as accessible and as affordable as economic circumstances permit. They frame this housing-led model of economic growth. The economy (and banks) needs large numbers of mortgaged households servicing debt and maintaining the cycle (and investment incentive) of house-price growth. Significant falls in the incomes needed to service loans, or big increases in monthly mortgage repayments because of rising interest rates, would stall the system, resulting in a recession in spending.

Lending practices and credit liberalisation have provided Harvey's 'fictional capital', needed ahead of actual production and consumption, enabling money capital to flow freely into fixed assets (Harvey, 1978: 107). That flow has produced unremitting house-price growth and new patterns of housing consumption: from domestic buyers moving their capital into bricks and mortar (and levering loans from rental income) to overseas buyers parking money in key investment destinations. Barker (2014: 14) makes the important point that the prospect of 'reasonable investment return' is a motivating factor in all private housing consumption. The investment motive is not new and underpins the preference for homeownership. But in some forms of consumption, the investment motive is more conspicuous and dominant.

There is currently burgeoning interest in foreign investment in globally connected cities – including London – not necessarily because that investment is seen as an overriding driver of national housing outcomes, but because it is emblematic of the change in the function of housing, and the way it is consumed, suggested above. That said, although foreign investment appears localised, there is now evidence that prices in the London housing market track investment behaviour to a greater extent than earnings (Meen, 2011). At the same time, the link with earnings has changed: whilst it makes intuitive sense that movement in workplace earnings should underpin housing demand and prices, the reality in recent years has been one of significant increases in house prices (a 41% increase since 2008 across the UK; ONS, 2016) running alongside declining workplace earnings (a drop of 10% in median real weekly earnings over the same period; Machin, 2015).

The decoupling of housing demand (and house prices) from earnings (in some areas) provides part of the evidence to suggest that the movement of wealth into housing is becoming a key market driver. But that wealth is not only sourced overseas. The purchase of second, third and further homes has been a feature of many Western housing markets for decades, motivated by the recreational opportunities and the investment potential that such purchases offer (Gallent et al, 2005; Paris, 2010). Amateur landlordism – manifest as *buy to let* in the UK – is also an important expression of housing's attraction to domestic investors beyond the asset growth that individual owner-occupiers enjoy. Although foreign buyers are also involved in this segment of the market, *buy to let* is principally a business or income supplement for UK buyers, some of whom worry about the future value of their pensions (Edwards, 2015) given the reliance of those pensions on the performance of stock market assets. The rapid expansion of amateur landlordism is a peculiarity of the UK housing system. This expansion began in the late 1980s with the creation of more flexible (and short-term) tenancy arrangements. Further deregulation of mortgage lending in the 1990s fuelled growth in the market. Today, a great many amateur landlords secure both capital appreciation and rental yields from *buy-to-let* property, pumping much of this new private wealth back into further housing consumption and investment, aiming to grow their portfolios and increase their profit take from housing.

The housing system in England and the rest of the UK – like many others – has been privatised in the later twentieth century. That privatisation has found support in credit liberalisation. The neoliberal project, as it pertains to housing, has been successful in shifting and broadening the function of housing, encouraging profit-taking from assets as a means of compensating for declining economic productivity. Support for homeownership – and more generally for private housing consumption – has morphed into support for the market through high-level fiscal policy and demand-side boosts, including recent initiatives such as *help to buy*. Housing has been recast as a market and economic good. Profit-taking (or *value extraction*) from fixed assets is a new economic cornerstone, vital to service-sector growth and the consumption of imported goods. Because of this economic role, the housing market has become untouchable. Government does not seek to control demand in any serious way (unless it clearly conflicts with growing homeownership, hence recent moves against *buy to let* and second homes). Rather, it deals with market externalities – including declining affordability – through specific product interventions, with these increasingly designed to support market access (hence the move from *social rents* to *affordable rents* and from part-ownership models to full-ownership *starter home* initiatives). Government's focus is on delivering market entry and asset ownership for the majority (as an economic priority and a vehicle for *asset-based welfare*) rather than working for broader access to decent homes. The worst-off households are placed in short-term accommodation, often in the private sector, with subsidy in the form of Housing Benefit directed to *buy to let* owners.

The planning system's role in all this is primarily to work for, and with, the market. Its focus is firmly on facilitating new build supply. *This means that its view of the housing crisis is incomplete and its reform or reorientation offers only a partial solution to a crisis that extends across the entire housing system and market.* For planning to be an answer to the housing crisis it would need to play a part in reshaping critical relationships. This important point is returned to at the end of this book.

The crisis for communities and people

The sense of crisis centred on the housing sector is expressed and amplified through the media: newspapers, television, the internet and, of course, social media all confirm the stress and distress arising from the inaccessibility of housing to key groups, especially the young (generally, aspiring buyers under 45) – the victims of a rising tide of intergenerational inequality centred on homeownership. The young today are far less likely to own their homes than young people 20 years ago (Resolution Foundation, 2018). They often find themselves, long term, in expensive rented accommodation that seldom meets their needs or expectations. Also, the commitment of a high proportion of their earnings to rent means that they are unable to save a deposit for a home of their own. The dream of homeownership drifts further away the longer they spend in rented accommodation, unless the 'bank of mum and dad' steps in and stumps up the cost of a deposit. This may happen for young people whose family background includes a history of property ownership. Parents may be able to release equity from their own homes or may simply have accumulated sufficient wealth that they are able to pass on. Intergenerational inequalities are hence fractured by inequalities arising from social background and family-based housing class. But, irrespective of such fractures, the young are clearly well represented within 'generation rent' and locked out of the many presented benefits of home ownership: stability, investment and the long-term advantage of seeing housing costs reduce as capital repayments eat into loan debt. Rather, they endure the instability of short-term tenancies without the tax efficiencies of homeownership (no tax on imputed rent) or rising equity (no tax on capital gain) in housing and suffering, instead, the threat of long-term increases in housing costs as rents rise faster than the rate of inflation. The prospects for generation rent, in the present rental market, are not good: workplace earnings unable to keep pace with housing costs and an inability to save for the future. These financial disadvantages then translate into a range of others stresses: a squeeze on family budgets and on quality of life as housing drains resources and prompts coping strategies that lead people to sign tenancy agreements on housing that in unsuited to their needs, either by virtue of location, price, quality or size. There is, of course, a spectrum of distress, ranging from the relatively light to the extraordinarily severe. On the 'lighter side' are the small compromises: houses sought in imperfect locations, which are not quite as spacious as one might have hoped, resulting in mild stresses in the home. Somewhere at the midpoint are homes dislocated from jobs, long morning and evening commutes, and resultant damage to home life. At a similar point on the spectrum, a different compromise between location and home might be reached, with families crammed into houses or flats far too small for their needs: children with no space in which to play or study, adults lacking privacy, and never the possibility of eating a meal together. At the far end are extreme situations in which low-quality rented housing, concentrated in poor neighbourhoods, is unfit for human habitation, being badly maintained and sometimes unsafe. Children and adults alike suffer poor health as a consequence, with housing seen as the crucial factor in eroding life chances. All scenarios across this full range of distress receive their share of media coverage. 'Hard-working families' for whom homeownership is just out of reach have been an important focus for the press. One key marker of their distress is the regular walk past the estate agents' window and the forlorn gaze at the purchase price of a three-bed semi. These are the target households for government's market access supports, including *help to buy*, its starter homes or changes to stamp duty. In the middle are the trials and tribulations of those in bad, but not life-threatening, housing. Dealings with inefficient lettings agents compound the challenges. A broken boiler left one letter-writer to *The Guardian* with 'no heating from January to March and showers at friends' (*The Guardian*, 2015a). The problem, as they saw it, was that 'landlords and agencies forget there are *real people* living in these houses and it is not just a case of making more money and trying to cut corners'. Households in the private rented sector are not a uniform group, but many will need more than market access support. They will be investigating shared equity options with housing associations or looking at radical solutions to their problems – a life away from London perhaps:

> In September we are moving from Hampshire to south Yorkshire. There is no other choice for us. And I am not moving because I necessarily want to buy a house – I am moving to be able to keep my family afloat, to not end up in a sea of debts and perhaps to start saving for a deposit. (*The Guardian*, 2015a)

Then there are those families in the very worst housing situations: renting privately from the successors to Perec 'Peter' Rachman, London's infamous and reputedly unscrupulous slum landlord. They will never benefit from market access support and lack the income even for the most generous shared equity schemes. Single people may end up in dreary bedsits, overcrowded rooms in private lodgings or converted garden sheds. Families fare little better, with children and adults sharing the same rooms in the worst cases. Where the housing is of slightly better quality, the compromise has been to accept relocation, sometimes hundreds of miles away, where all family and friendship ties are lost. Wandsworth Borough Council's policy of offering its tenants the chance to relocate out of London came under media scrutiny a few years ago, with one councillor arguing that:

> It's wrong to pressure local families to leave Battersea to move to Birmingham ... These really are some of our most vulnerable tenants, you can either help them improve their lives or you can try and ship them out of the area and get some different people in. (*The Guardian*, 2015b)

Moving forward

The quotes above invoke ideas of family, stability and the needs of 'real people'. They speak to the communal, social, purpose of housing. In this chapter, I have alluded to the economic and asset function of housing and the complexities of a market which is called on to deliver both homes and opportunities for wealth extraction from residential property. I have also introduced the book's main contention: that the housing system's diminishing capacity to perform its social purpose – to provide access to decent homes at a reasonable cost – is a result of individuals' and economies' changing relationship with land and property. That changed relationship – and increased reliance on the built environment as a source of wealth or value extraction – is at the root of global housing crises, which occasionally erupt before *seemingly* fading away. At a structural level, financial markets have invented new ways of extracting profit from land and fixed assets, bringing housing into the permanent circuits of capital accumulation. This leads to a demand for development (beyond utility) dominated by the needs of capital rather than people, and an associated growth of financial and real estate services that form an increasingly large part of the national economy. Lower down, individuals are locked into an increasingly complex relationship with land and housing: indirectly, the value of private pensions is dependent on the upward trajectory of property prices; more directly, these individuals are often investors themselves, with their homes (primary, secondary and so on) held as assets against which personal finance can be raised during their lifetime (therefore becoming a source of consumer confidence and consumption, linking back to a wider economic relationship), a hedge against poorly performing public and private pensions and a pot of wealth that can be transferred to the next generation – often in support of home purchase.

The analysis in this book will inevitably be incomplete. It would be odd to present the housing crisis as an outcome of immense complexity before calmly slicing through *all* of that complexity and arriving at complete answers. I offer a partial view, focused around consumption and the question of *what housing is for*, and general readers or reviewers will quickly find its blind spots. Equally, they will point out that housing stress has a spatial and cyclical patterning. Not everywhere is like London and, over time, prices rise and fall. Homes in Worcester, Burnley or Hastings invariably cost less to buy or rent, relative to earnings, than equivalent homes in Wandsworth, Barnet or Hemel Hempstead. At the opposite extreme of the housing crisis examined in this book are those situations where asset has become liability, and where low-income owner occupation in 'left-behind places' has become the defining measure of housing stress. There are certainly alternative facets – *other housing crises* that warrant their own analysis – to the one examined in this book, but irrespective of place or time, our underlying relationship with housing, flagged above, remains the same – giving rise to spatial and cyclical eruptions that have underlying, albeit occasionally dormant, causes. Indeed, we are moving from a situation, some decades ago, in which periodic crises of capitalism saw the temporary transfer of surplus capital into housing, to a situation today in which the secondary circuit has acquired greater permanence as financial markets and instruments more readily mediate the flow of capital to and from housing.

Whose Housing Crisis? relays the story of housing in England in six chapters. This opening chapter has noted outward manifestations of the crisis: spiralling housing costs relative to earnings and a generation locked out of the market. In passing, it has explored what I have termed the housing/planning nexus, focusing on what constitutes 'supply' and planning's role in facilitating new housing production. More importantly, it has sketched the reasons for capital movements to, and investment in, housing. It has presented these as being central to the housing crisis. The next chapter (2) explores the inherent complexity of housing processes and outcomes, arguing that, in sum, they present analysts and policy makers with the definitive 'wicked problem': a problem that is symptomatic of a deeper crisis, which has been reached by multiple paths and from which there is no easy exit. Chapters 3 and 4 then contain the main parts of my analysis, dealing first with housing's economic context and the drivers that underpin housing outcomes, and second with the local pathways that have brought us to the particular challenges faced in England and across the rest of the UK. Chapter 4, in particular, shows how these pathways have intersected over time and how the main formulations of the housing crisis (centred on supply, credit, investment, marketisation and so on) are all part of the same complete narrative. Chapter 5 then turns to the book's titular question – Whose housing crisis? – and argues that growth, outside of the real economy, is not delivering either shared prosperity or sustainable development. Rather, it is producing gross inequality and a critical loss of social cohesion, particularly between generations. The crisis is therefore deep and pervasive, affecting everyone sooner or later. Finally, Chapter 6 does what every book on the housing crisis needs to do: it attempts to formulate an exit strategy. That strategy separates interim measures (and an element of backtracking up the different paths that have led to crisis), from those aimed at addressing the problematic assets/homes relationship. It identifies tax and credit for housing consumption as areas of critical concern. It also acknowledges the 'dual' nature of the housing market by proposing a new approach to planning which supports the *right to a stable and secure home* over the right to property ownership.

2

A wicked problem

Housing – or, more specifically, achieving broader equality of access to housing – is a *wicked problem*. The purpose of this chapter is to explain why, and also to show how the anatomy of the housing crisis shares many, if not all, of the core characteristics of such a problem. The housing stresses briefly introduced in the last chapter are generally thought to have complicated underlying causes: there are big structural reasons why housing is currently at the centre of a far-reaching social and economic crisis, and there are also numerous local paths that have brought England and other parts of the UK to this predicament. An attempt to plot those local paths is made in Chapter 4. The inherent complexity of the housing system, and the multitude of ways in which critical pathways cross and interact to produce particular housing outcomes, have given the crisis its intractable quality. Politicians have occasionally flagged some of that complexity, including former Chancellor George Osborne, in his much-quoted 2014 Mansion House Speech:

> 'For most people, their home is the biggest investment of their lifetime. And, of course, they want that asset to increase in value over time. But a home is also a place to live and build our lives – and we want all families to be able to afford security, comfort and peace of mind. That means homes have to be affordable – whether you're renting or buying. The only way that can be achieved over the long term is by building more, so supply better matches demand. But we are a small and crowded island, keen to protect our green spaces and ready to object to new development. So the British people want our homes to go up in value, but also remain affordable; and we want more homes built, just not next to us. You can see why no one has managed yet to solve the problems of Britain's housing market.'

But complex problems do not necessarily defy resolution. Rather, there is some hope that clever people will dedicate themselves to unravelling those problems and solve them in the end. *Social* problems, however, embedded deeply within the cultural and political lives of different societies, often have a level of complexity that makes them more than merely difficult to decode. For such wicked problems, 'there are no *solutions* in the sense of definitive and objective answers' (Rittel and Webber, 1973: 155), as the outcomes those problems generate are not definitively or objectively good or bad. The current housing system, for example, looks to be good (enough) for existing homeowners and investors who benefit from long-term rises in house prices. Falling prices could be good for prospective buyers, but only if those falls are not linked to economic stagnation, reduced job opportunities and a drop in earnings. There are two problems: good outcomes may be a mirror to bad outcomes, given the complexity of the system, and, more importantly, judgements as to whether something is good or bad are subject to market position. Notwithstanding the economic complexities, soaring *or* plummeting prices are subjectively good outcomes, but neither outcome will have wholly benign consequences. Wicked problems are not merely complex but display resistance to resolution.

The general notion of social problems as wicked problems, distinct from the *tame problems* of science, was introduced by Horst Rittel in a seminar attended by his University of California, Berkeley, colleague, C. West Churchman, in 1967 (Churchman, 1967: B141). Then Rittel, in collaboration with Melvin Webber, presented a full exploration of the nature of wicked problems in the journal *Policy Sciences*, in 1973. Their paper, 'Dilemmas in a general theory of planning', has since garnered a significant number of citations (almost 12,200 by July 2018) and has been used to frame analyses of many social problems. It has been used specifically in relation to housing on several thousand occasions. Housing development in England has been viewed as a wicked problem (Adams, 2011) and so has housing market renewal and demolition (Cole, 2012): intervening in the supply of housing, through different planning approaches, brings us into a subjective world, where there are often no wrong or right answers.

How the concept is used in analysis of housing and other problems varies considerably. Sometimes it is merely another label for systemic complexity, ahead of the claim that a problem can be objectively solved. 'Dilemmas in a general theory of planning' is open to varied interpretation. Coming out of the 1960s, it rejects systems analysis (and the systems approach in planning) and its presentation of optimum solutions. Coming out of Berkeley, California, it can also be read as a rejection of expertise and orchestrated top-down solutions to the challenges of neighbourhoods. But the paper is not a defence of localism; although it can be read as being supportive of local resolution aligned to the priorities of local publics, the substitution of 'expert professional judgement for those of contending political groups may make the rationales and the repercussions more explicit, but it would not necessarily make the outcomes better' (Rittel and Webber, 1973: 169). The main contribution of Rittel and Webber's 1973 paper is not to flag easy answers but rather to reveal the characteristics – or the anatomy – of wicked social problems. Housing problems share that anatomy and there is, therefore, value in presenting the housing crisis as a wicked problem in order to better understand its nature, its drivers and some of the actions that might alleviate its symptoms (short of a complete systemic shift that unseats the entire capitalist model of production).

The 'inherent wickedness' (Rittel and Webber, 1973: 161) of social problems can be read in their ten main characteristics:

1. There is no definitive formulation of a wicked problem.
2. Wicked problems have no stopping rule.
3. Solutions to wicked problems are not true or false, but good or bad.
4. There is no immediate and no ultimate test of a solution to a wicked problem.
5. Every solution to a wicked problem is a 'one-shot operation'; because there is no opportunity to learn by trial and error, every attempt counts significantly.
6. Wicked problems do not have an enumerable (or an exhaustively describable) set of potential solutions, nor is there a well-described set of permissible operations that may be incorporated into the plan.
7. Every wicked problem is essentially unique.
8. Every wicked problem can be considered to be a symptom of another problem.
9. The existence of a discrepancy representing a wicked problem can be explained in numerous ways. The choice of explanation determines the nature of the problem's resolution.
10. The social planner has no right to be wrong (that is, planners are liable for the consequences of the actions they generate).

Housing as a wicked problem

In the last chapter, I argued that the housing crisis, despite its spatial and cyclical ebbs and flows, has underlying causes that are constant and hardwired into the social and economic life of England and the rest of the UK. In the sections that follow, the ten characteristics of wicked problems described 45 years ago are compared with characteristics of the housing crisis. All are pertinent but three are picked out for greater scrutiny in the next three chapters of this book: the housing crisis is fixed within a larger economic canvas (8); there are multiple pathways to (and explanations of) that crisis – and belief in the overriding importance of one will determine the preferred response (9); and, given the subjectivity of interpretation (3), any solution will inevitably be 'better or worse' rather than true or false. What will emerge from this chapter are four further chapters that set housing problems within the context of economic change, track pathways and formulations, examine the subjectivity of interpretation by asking who is affected by the crisis and related housing and economic outcomes, and examine better or worse solutions.

(1) The reality of there being *no definitive formulation of a wicked problem* seems self-evident in relation to housing. This book proposes an anatomy of the housing crisis which prioritises particular features: it offers a formulation that emphasises distorted economic and social relationships, and that formulation '*is* the problem'. 'The process of formulating the problem and of conceiving a solution (or re-resolution) are identical, since every specification of the problem is a specification of the direction in which a treatment is considered' (Rittel and Webber, 1973: 161). This process results in a constrained 'solution space' (p. 162), largely because, in this instance, I view housing as a social good, the delivery of which is disrupted by a switch of capital into property, leading to a refunctioning of housing. If, on the other hand, housing were viewed as infrastructure and a public good, then the prescribed solution would surely be the channelling of public funding into an enlarged infrastructure programme that included housing (removing housing from *the market*, if that were possible and if public housing were not subject to the same forces of financialisation as private housing). The admission that formulation is itself problematic, and often limited, is merely to concede subjectivity. But government's view that "the only way that [affordability] can be achieved over the long term is by building more [houses], so supply better matches demand" points to an arguably more limited, and politically constrained, formulation, leading to a simple answer (build more houses) that fails to address the inherent wickedness of the problem. More nuanced understandings of the housing crisis are needed, which acknowledge the interconnections that frame better or worse answers. In defence of my own prescription, it a) looks

beyond land use regulation as the cause of low affordability, and b) acknowledges broader economic linkages.

(2) It is difficult to think of any social problem that has been definitively *solved*, and it is equally difficult to imagine that the housing crisis can be brought to an abrupt end – that there is a *stopping rule*. Housing stress is a dimension of poverty (even for better-off families whose earnings are inadequate relative to housing costs). When this book eventually reaches its prescriptions for easing that stress, and bringing the price paid for housing closer to the earnings of ordinary families in different parts of the country, it will not have solved anything, but simply suggested means of alleviating stress. Its proposition is that housing can be made more affordable: that people do not need to live with the burden of excessive debt and that economies can be weaned off reliance on the extraction of financial income from housing. But its prescriptions are for a general market in which the social function of housing is restored, while acknowledging that 'there are no ends to the causal chains that link interacting open systems' and that the 'would-be planner can always try to do better' (Rittel and Webber, 1973: 162).

The aim is to make some headway, at least in an analytical sense: to contribute to a better understanding of housing outcomes. But it is difficult to conceive of housing stress being brought to an end by any single action. Formulations that see reduced regulation as a means of delivering optimised welfare through the market do not envisage *universalised* welfare: all housing needs being met by that market. Rather, they see an optimum outcome extending to a great many households but with some still requiring assistance – helped by a welfare 'safety net'. But deregulation, especially affecting financial markets, creates additional demand for consumption (aiding the movement of capital into the secondary circuit) and places new pressures on the existing stock while driving demand for further development. As one housing problem is 'solved' (costs start to realign with earnings), another is created as demand for additional housing space pushes up against environmental and political limits. Likewise, formulations that see more households renting (and reduced reliance on homeownership) point to the benefits of new institutional investment in a stable, professional rental sector. Young people are sold the idea that renting from specialist companies will deliver reduced costs (removing the need for a large deposit), flexibility (to move without significant transaction costs) and the stability of longer rental contracts (with periodic break clauses that do not result in rent hikes). Real estate investment trusts (REITs) supporting new rental models are, however, another vehicle through which capitalists can switch capital to the built environment and extract profit. They are a housing 'solution' (for some) that does not address underlying inequality arising from the concentration of property in fewer hands (see figures presented in Chapter 5). It often serves capitalist production to narrowly define the housing problem (it is about young people in unstable situations, spending too high a proportion of their income on rents/mortgages) and then arrive at solutions that maintain the underlying status quo. Even solutions that rely on increased public intervention (by allowing the local state to borrow and build new 'council housing') are today situated in a system reliant on financial markets and investors. Council housing is part of the consumption fund: loans are held by banks and may be securitised, sold on to investors who derive financial income from a mix of rents and public subsidy directed at this 'non-market housing' which, nonetheless, delivers income through financial markets.

All of these solutions are political *projects* undertaken within a broader 'interacting open system' that produces the built environment and housing outcomes. While that system continues to operate, it acts to limit the extent to which particular actions effect change. Deregulation (rolling back land-use planning and/or the constraints on new investors entering the market) and building more council houses are presented as ideologically opposed answers to the housing crisis. But both work with the same underlying system and enlarging the stock of council homes will itself require deregulation, giving financial markets greater access to the public sector, enabling the latter to borrow and build.

(3) None of these answers, therefore, deal with underlying inequality which is structured by the control of property and debt. They are 'good enough' (Rittel and Webber, 1973: 162) responses, depending on one's ideological predilection. Indeed, the third marker of a wicked problem is that no answer is itself definitive. Rather, it is 'good' or 'bad' depending on the special interest in which it is rooted or the value set that frames it. Increasing the general supply of new homes for purchase has broadest appeal, appearing to serve the interests and aspirations of private and institutional investors; REITs (that support professional renting) are a new investment vehicle that may win support among households locked in unstable renting, while preserving established capital circuits; and council housing ostensibly challenges the power of the market, and therefore wins plaudits on the political left. These are just three examples of actions (many others could be presented) and they are all good enough for someone, depending on their value set, market position, political leaning and so on.

But while accepting that there is no definitive answer owing to the open-ended nature of the system, it seems likely that by identifying where interests converge it will be possible to plot a solution that commands broad appeal. Many existing solutions to housing stress are predicated on the belief that those stresses are narrowly felt and do not produce broader repercussions. The same is true of inequality and poverty: they are commonly presented as socially specific rather than systemic, rippling through societies and economies. That presentation is itself interest-driven (avoiding the need to do more, change behaviour, redirect spending and so on), but if those interests were to accept a much broader account of the impacts arising from housing stress and inequality, viewing that stress – for example – as a fundamental threat to capital accumulation, and therefore growth, then the need to act decisively might gain broader support. But Harvey (1978) and also Piketty (2014) observe that the capitalist class seldom pursues 'class interest', but rather the self-interest achieved through competitive advantage – if others turn aside from the pursuit of simple profit then this will hand competitive advantage to those who stay the course. Proof of this is found in responses to climate science. Despite overwhelming evidence of the anthropogenic causes of worsening climatic conditions, some governments (and the corporate interests that support them) argue that growth (which is considered essential) can only be achieved through faster exploitation of natural resources, generating the environmental pollution and pollutants that the vast majority of scientists link to the sorts of climate shifts that could ultimately bring environmental, social and economic chaos. If *sustainable development* has failed to gain traction as a prerequisite for prosperity, what hope is there that *social equality* (with *social inequality* being shown, in Chapter 5, to be a core driver of unsustainable development) will fare any better?

Despite the power of self-interest, a great many people in the world today accept the need to act in ways that reduce damage to the planet. Many governments are pursuing targets for the reduction of CO2 emissions and many corporations ascribe to modes of environmental behaviour that their customers deem important. Although the capitalist class will pursue self-interest, the focus of that interest will shift if it is widely accepted that inequality is generating fundamental systemic risk rather than surface outcomes that can be ignored. Any case for serious change must be grounded in an assessment of the scope and depth of the problem which that change seeks to address.

(4) 'With wicked problems ... any solution, after being implemented, will generate waves of consequences over an extended – virtually an

unbounded – period of time' (Rittel and Webber, 1973: 163). If one accepts that the housing crisis is hardwired into the processes of capital accumulation and deregulation of financial markets (producing and facilitating investment and credit flows that disrupt the relationship between housing costs and earnings), one also has to accept that serious intervention is likely to have far-reaching consequences. Indeed, 'the next day's consequences of the solution may yield utterly undesirable repercussions which outweigh the intended advantages' (p. 163). In light of the complexity of linkages, surface solutions seem perfectly justified: it is better to address a narrow set of symptoms (market supports for aspiring homeowners or a limited programme of public housebuilding for the poorest households) than risk big economic disruptions. But such is the complexity of the system that even surface solutions generate waves of repercussions. In November 2017, stamp duty on homes costing less than £300,000 was removed for first-time buyers. The Office for Budget Responsibility observed that this particular 'market support' will mean that house prices will be 0.3% higher in a year's time than they would otherwise have been. Such interventions (cuts in transaction taxes or other forms of purchase assistance for target groups) generate their own price inflation, delivering price benefits only for those buyers who take advantage of them within the first few months. If the intention is to support housing access then the efficacy of such interventions is doubtful; if, on the other hand, the aim is to keep house prices on their upward track, then they appear to be very effective. The overall level of homeownership in England has fallen, but the housing market remains 'buoyant' (see Chapter 4). Surface solutions generally have controllable, or at least predictable, impacts despite the underlying complexity of the problems they purport to address. Hence, to cautious and conservative governments they are acceptable: little incremental steps that are not too disruptive and which satisfy key interests. In the case of stamp duty, the loss of public revenue during the early months of implementation will be recovered in later years as prices are pushed onto a higher track.

Although housing (or, more precisely, greater equality of access to housing) is clearly a wicked problem, it is such a fundamental problem – embedded in processes of capital accumulation and questions of equality – that, as noted above, it is difficult to conceive of a decisive response (targeting the roots of the problem) that would command broad support and not result in a shock wave of social and economic disruptions. Given the entrenched nature of the housing crisis, it might seem sensible (and politic) to respond to outward symptoms, accepting that those responses should be narrow in scope and targeted.

Does this mean that the housing problem is different from a regular wicked problem and should be broken down into components – the planning problem, the new supply problem, the welfare housing challenge and so on? These individual components have already been separated out and presented as wicked problems in their own right (see Adams, 2011). But the huge complexity – and potential 'waves of consequences' – of acting on the 'housing system' (and its connections to land and economic systems) does not mean that such broader actions are not possible. Patterns of land ownership (and hence the capture of land rents) and regulations affecting capital markets support different housing outcomes in different countries. Outcomes in England are the culmination of a century of political decisions – this is illustrated in Chapter 4, where the various 'local pathways to crisis' are plotted. Despite the cumulative effect of those decisions, decisive actions are possible, effecting changes to land owners' rights and the way that capital markets are regulated, which could transform the function of housing. However, the more pervasive issue here – which is returned to under (8) below – is that housing's importance in Harvey's secondary circuit gives it an economic function that cannot be understated (as consumption fund and an engine of 'wealth creation'). Any and all actions that target the root of the housing *access* crisis will impact on the wider economy, acting irreversibly on peoples' lives in a variety of ways. This issue is picked up again in Chapter 6 where proposals for fundamental change, which seek to alter the asset function of all or some housing, are either implemented gradually (to lessen economic disruption) or accompanied with preparatory or parallel actions that could otherwise make them practicable.

(5) Rittel and Webber (1973) drew an important distinction between the 'inconsequential' outcomes of 'trial and error' in response to closed-system 'tame problems', compared with the longevity of impacts arising from implemented solutions to open-system social problems. An experiment in controlled conditions can tell the scientist whether a particular action will have a desired result, without having broader ramifications. Planning interventions, on the other hand, are presented as 'one-shot operations' that impact on the subsequent 'course of societal affairs'. In this respect, the authors envisaged physical changes (for example, new roads) impacting on places and on people, which might not easily be adjusted. Experimental runs were viewed as a luxury of scientific enquiry. In relation to housing, interventions (ahead of building the housing) are not necessarily physical and the consequences of systemic intervention can be modelled using technologies with a level of sophistication not envisaged almost half a

century ago. Indeed, the impacts of regulatory adjustment on growth, tax yield and (house) prices is regularly modelled by the Office for Budget Responsibility (see above). Models are being developed to explain and project the impact of economic and regulatory change on house prices, affordability and access (see, for example, Dianati et al, 2017), but policy adjustments are seldom informed (or practically constrained) by open-system modelling. Ideology, conviction and the trialling of ideas are far more important. *Help to buy* has been lambasted as 'help to bubble' (Dorling, 2015: 175), with evidence pointing to its role in elevating house prices. It is, however, effective in helping households on the cusp of homeownership onto the 'housing ladder' and thereafter keeping prices on an upward track. It is a market support rather than a social support.

Models are subject to interpretation: do those commissioning, producing or observing the model view weakening or strengthening price growth as a good thing? Similarly, models rarely capture all inputs or feedback loops and, at some point, there needs to be an element of trial. Supported by political conviction, such trials quickly become policy – interventions in the real world that 'leave traces that cannot be undone' (Rittel and Webber, 1973: 163). Traces of past intervention provide the foundations for the current housing crisis: the supply of non-market affordable housing was decimated by the decision to sell it to sitting tenants; deregulation of mortgage markets (Stephens, 2007; Wainwright, 2009) accelerated the flow of credit into private housing, causing a spiralling of housing prices; and, even further back, the decision to nationalise development rights, rather than nationalise the ownership of land, has sustained a situation in which land rents are captured primarily by landowners and the planning system struggles to exert its will on development outcomes.

One might add that the current triad of *land–planning–development* debates is anchored more deeply in the idea of *private property*. Private ownership of land is an obstacle that the planning system struggles to navigate, but planning, rather than ownership, is more commonly presented as the problem to solve. This is because private interest/ownership of land is generally accepted to be a 'natural state' and planning an artificial intrusion. However, there is nothing natural or unnatural about private, collective or state ownership of land – all that can be said is that the dogged defence of private property in Western society has left a heavy imprint (traces) on patterns of social and economic advantage and inequality.

(6) The complexity of this imprint (of observable traces and their origins) hints at another fundamental characteristic of wicked

problems: the range of conceivable solutions is enormous and not 'exhaustively describable' (Rittel and Webber, 1973: 164). This is due to both the complexity of the open system in which the problem is situated (or of which it is an integral part) and the vast range of interests that will support single or combined actions or support no action at all, viewing the status quo as optimal. 'There are no criteria which enable one to prove that all solutions to a wicked problem have been identified and considered' (Rittel and Webber, 1973: 164). Moreover, 'logical inconsistencies' (between different goals or priorities – see Osborne's comment on the housing crisis at the beginning of this chapter) may result in 'no solution' being found. Also, *judgement* is so fundamental to actions in the social world – judgement underpinned by a particular value set or other predilections – that the range of options will regularly be curtailed by 'practical limits' placed (by a powerful individual or group) on that range. In relation to housing access, there has been an oscillation in England between general inaction, piecemeal tinkering (mainly with the planning system, in response to an acceptance that protracted public tests slow new housing output) and limited backtracking (towards non-market housing solutions). Political judgement, however, generally constrains permissible 'strategies-or-moves'. Possible responses to everyday 'street crime' (in the US) are used by Rittel and Webber to illustrate the inexhaustible nature of options:

> Which strategies-or-moves are permissible in dealing with crime in the streets, for example, have been enumerated nowhere. 'Anything goes,' or at least, any new idea for a planning measure may become a serious candidate for a re-solution: what should we do to reduce street crime? Should we disarm the police, as they do in England, since even criminals are less likely to shoot unarmed men? Or repeal the laws that define crime, such as those that make marijuana use a criminal act or those that make car theft a criminal act? That would reduce crime by changing definitions. Try moral rearmament and substitute ethical self-control for police and court control? Shoot all criminals and thus reduce the numbers who commit crime? Give away free loot to would-be-thieves, and so reduce the incentive to crime? And so on. (Rittel and Webber, 1973: 164)

This list does not extend to interventions that view surface problems as being rooted in deeper crises. Street crime is symptomatic of social inequalities, which are in turn underpinned by economic processes, which are in turn grounded in the pattern of control of resources. The list could therefore extend into social and economic policy or interventions that redistribute resources or shift them into collective or state ownership. Housing access shares this characteristic: some of the mooted and actual solutions from England are remarkably similar to Rittel and Webber's responses to street crime. Housing affordability is the critical barrier to housing access, but big structural obstacles stand in the way of making private housing generally more affordable. Preference has therefore been given to producing a special class of 'affordable housing', initially using direct state subsidy and later by capturing an element of the land value uplift generated when market housing is permissioned (Crook et al, 2016). The latter strategy, however, failed to match affordable housing supply to demand. Government responded by changing definitions – calling 'market discount' housing, produced with a smaller element of planning gain, 'affordable housing'. The percentage of affordable housing being delivered promptly rose: but in the same way that decriminalising car theft will not reduce the number of cars being stolen, a *redefinition* of what constitutes affordable housing will not widen housing access. Likewise, 'moral rearmament' finds a parallel in government's preference for self-help, its faith in neoliberal policy and its aversion to public sector intervention. Yet while there are similarities across all social problems, the processes underpinning those problems are 'essentially unique' (Rittel & Webber, 1973: 164) even if they regularly share a rootedness in broader systems.

(7) Outward similarities between problems pose a risk to policy makers and planners: the risk of jumping to quick conclusions and easy answers. Housing access can be grouped with other 'welfare', 'infrastructure', 'planning', 'social equity' or, indeed, 'economic' problems. That grouping can be used to justify fast answers centred on increased spending, deregulation, redistribution or tighter regulation. Likewise, housing problems can appear similar from one country to another, rather than being destinations that are reached via different structural and local pathways. It is important to plot those pathways and question the proposed application of one country's answers to another country's problems. We come, therefore, to a significant truism, which seems particularly pertinent to England's housing crisis: 'part of the art of dealing with wicked problems is the art of not knowing too early which type of solutions to apply' (Rittel & Webber, 1973: 163). The pressure to act is of course enormous. England's housing crisis is viewed as a long-incubated problem resulting, as some would have

it, from the incompetence of the planning system and the greed of developers. People's lives are being blighted by poor housing; there is an urgent need to 'mobilise across the nation to build the homes our children need' (the sub-title of the Lyons Report; Lyons, 2014) and there is the potential for electoral gain for anyone who can make inroads towards resolution, or even just pinpoint causes and actions that are electorally popular.

The most popular are, of course, attacks on 'bureaucracy', on housebuilders who have failed in their 'duty to Britain' (BBC News, 2018a) and the suggestion that councils should step in and provide affordable homes. Politicians have been careful to steer the public away from demand-side arguments, particularly the role of foreign investors in driving up house prices in London. Reporting on the alleged attempt by Russian agents to assassinate Sergei Skripal in March 2018, the BBC's James Landale speculated that, in response, 'the UK could make it more difficult for Russians generally to get visas to the UK' but that such action might not be in the country's interests as 'such restrictions might also hit … wealthy businessmen whose laundered cash the UK tolerates to support London's property market' (BBC News, 2018b). It was noted earlier that keeping prices on their upward track is profoundly important for the UK: 'support for the property market' (homes 'going up in value') seems often to trump homes 'remaining affordable'. These goals are not viewed as divergent, but the trick is how to achieve both within a housing/planning system that makes no distinction between homes (for 'working families') and assets (for capital accumulation and for economic support). This issue is returned to in the final pages of this book.

The scramble for fast answers is also driven by a plethora of think tanks whose reputations depend on their ability to spin out branded solutions to the housing crisis. Over at least the last twenty years, governments on the left and right have been advised by policy gurus (and seldom academics) who are in the *business* of developing showpiece policies that governments can promote and roll out: ideas that will deliver political capital. For example, Local Place Partnerships – 'a set of new locally-led bodies that can offer the ecosystem of support needed to overcome the barriers faced in the delivery, funding and planning of the scale of new homes and infrastructure we need' (Fagleman, 2015: 4) – have been proposed, and these seek to cast local authorities as 'coordinators' of development. This idea from ResPublica was, with some tweaks, a composite of previous approaches (Labour's Special Delivery Vehicles for the growth areas, the Coalition Government's Housing Zones and Urban Development

Corporations). It was, however, a new thing with a new badge, with its proponent taking a dim view of the local authority planning function – implying that authorities were not already coordinators of development/change, through their forward planning and development management functions and through their established relationships with private enterprise and third sector partners. But new things are useful, giving the impression that governments are not bereft of ideas and are proactive in seeking solutions. Think tanks work with the short-termism of politics, with the rhythms of democracy and with the enthusiasm of elected politicians to find answers that can be delivered within a single parliament and return quick political capital. Governments work with those think tanks that share their ideals, and some of them have extremely close links with particular political parties: indeed, the boundary between internal and external advice is often blurred and ministers work with their 'preferred suppliers' of branded ideas. Politics demands that the 'right' actions are known, and taken, early on. Likewise, answers that are disruptive in the short to medium term but deliver long-term benefit are unlikely to be actioned – the party in power would pay the political price while the rewards could end up in the hands of its opposition. Barker (2014) observes this in relation to property tax reform: new taxes (or application of existing ones in new ways – including capital gains tax on primary residences) might help reduce the attractiveness of housing relative to other asset classes, but such a move would be hugely unpopular and voters would be slow to forgive the party that inflicted this pain. Careful calculation and long-termism are rarely features of the policy/political process, making it difficult to address complex, wicked problems that are deeply entrenched in a broadly accepted political economy.

The nature of the housing crisis has only been revealed through the rhythms of the market. Harvey's capital switches have become more pronounced, aided by deregulation and maturation of financial markets, with bubbles more readily inflating and – in some locations at least – staying inflated for longer as capital finds a more permanent home in housing and other forms of property (these issues are dealt with at length in the next chapter). For capital, the aforementioned 'clever people' have already found some solutions to their housing crisis: new financial instruments have made property more liquid and new ways have been invented to derive financial income from debt. It is indebted households and not banks/investors (who retain assets following loan default) who feel the brunt of downturns – assuming the latter have shown some prudency in their lending practices. A system that has been long in the making, and in which critical relationships with housing are embedded, will be slow to change – and can only be changed through a long-term programme of interventions, as opposed to fast actions that address surface problems.

(8) 'The higher the level of a problem's formulation, the broader and more general it becomes: and the more difficult it becomes to do something about it. On the other hand, one should not try to cure symptoms: and therefore one should try to settle the problem on as high a level as possible' (Rittel and Webber, 1973: 165). The short-termism of parliamentary democracy demands a focus on curing symptoms: disruptive consumption of housing arises from its transformation into asset – therefore, build more houses, or at least be seen to make credible strides in this direction (thereby offsetting the effects of excessive consumption for as many voting households as possible). A steady stream of commentators have situated housing in broader crises and problems, starting with Friedrich Engels: 'as long as the capitalist mode of production continues to exist, it is folly to hope for an *isolated solution* of the housing question or of any other social question affecting the fate of the workers' (Engels, 1872 [1970]: 71). More recent contributions have similarly dismissed 'isolated' or incremental actions. Housing, for Piketty (2014), is central to his analysis of inequality and low productivity, but it is market processes (and function) that generate those outcomes. Indeed, in their analysis of the implications of Piketty's *Capital in the Twenty-first Century* for the more prosaic matter of public policy, Maclennan and Miao (2017: 127) argue that 'housing market processes and wealth outcomes will drive higher inequality and lower productivity into the future unless housing and related policies change markedly'. Housing is placed at the heart of economic debates, but it is the political economy in which housing is positioned (and the treatment of housing in financial markets) that is responsible for generating particular local outcomes. Broadly the same observation is made by Ryan-Collins and colleagues (2012) who explore how banks 'create' money on their balance sheets when advancing loans on property: that process of money creation has swollen what was once a trickle of credit into housing into a flood. It was made possible through deregulation – a feature of 'mature financial markets' that aids the switch of capital into the secondary circuit (Harvey, 1978). In another contribution led by Ryan-Collins, the centrality of *land* to the housing question is flagged (Ryan-Collins et al, 2017): private ownership of land is pivotal to capitalist production, being a fundamental source of wealth creation through the capture of land rents. When land is in private ownership, those rents flow directly to owners/investors and, unless some clever

way is found to capture them, they will be lost to society at large – or, more particularly, to the public sector, which might otherwise use them to pay for infrastructure or more effectively control the use of land for wider social benefit.

All of these accounts of the housing crisis (marked by its access inequalities and stresses) share an acknowledgment that the extraction of profit, and pursuit of greater wealth, through housing (and land) bear great responsibility for socioeconomic outcomes. The accounts share other characteristics as well: they lean (to varying degrees) towards Marxian analysis and none view incrementalism as offering adequate or lasting answers to observed problems. Rather, answers on a seismic scale are presented: 'abolition of the capitalist mode of production', a 'global wealth tax' or 'land value tax' in lieu of a transfer of land out of private ownership. Such high-level answers would be difficult to implement. For that reason, or more usually because of short-termism and vested interest, the 'doctrine [of incrementalism] advertises a policy of small steps, in the hope of contributing systematically to overall improvement. If, however, the problem is attacked on too low a level (an increment), then success of resolution may result in making things worse, because it may become more difficult to deal with the higher problems' (Rittel and Webber, 1973: 165). Housing policy in England would appear to offer a good example of this: as more people, on average or even unstable incomes, are helped into private homeownership (through the *right to buy*, *help to buy*, stamp duty cuts and so forth) through a brokered relationship with the banks, the proportion of the population dependent on house price growth rises. Housing, for many, becomes their biggest investment – and to remain confident consumers, they need to see that investment grow, and will therefore reject any reforms that appear to threaten their personal finances. Housing policy has widened dependence on the underlying 'system' in a way that Engels may never have imagined. In *The Housing Question*, he mocked the idea that 'workers' could 'become capitalists' by acquiring 'their own little houses'. 'Capital', he declares 'is the command over the unpaid labour of others. The little house of the worker can therefore become capital only if he rents it to a third person and appropriates a part of the labour product of this third person in the form of rent' (Engels, 1872 [1970]: 46). The broadening of homeownership in the twentieth century and its extension into amateur landlordism in England has brought more people into the 'capitalist' ranks; although a recent decline in the overall level of homeownership, as more people struggle to buy property, perhaps signals the opening of a window through which it will be possible to build consensus for more than just 'small steps'. The intention here has been to offer just a glimpse of a wider panorama (how the housing problem is 'a symptom of another problem') that is more fully revealed in the next chapter and which is also localised to England and the UK.

(9) Within that wider panorama, there have been multiple 'pathways' along which the housing crisis has been reached. These can be viewed as formulations (see 1 above) or explanations that fit a particular analyst's world view. That world view is generally the 'strongest determining factor in explaining [a] wicked problem' (Rittel and Webber, 1973: 166). The plausibility attached to a particular explanation will depend, of course, on positionality (and interest), ideological predilection and also the knowledge (and disciplinary) base of the observer. Causes are looked for, by different observers, in the fields of economics and finance, social and public policy, political science and so on. However, it seems to me that with a problem as big as housing affordability and access, explanations are unlikely to be mutually exclusive and particular narrative paths will be parts of a more complete story in which those paths interact and intersect. Likewise, many disciplines have contributions to make to the analysis of housing outcomes. Housing as a topic of enquiry locates at the intersection between political, economic, moral and ethical concerns. High-end conspicuous consumption of housing in many world cities supports, through tax contribution and spending, both the 'property market' and a wider economic ecosystem (Hilber and Schöni, 2018). But that pattern of consumption, and the economic processes that underpin it, produce inequalities in quality of life and life chances that surely present moral and ethical questions – or not, depending on the position and interest of the observer. These questions aside, 'the choice of explanation [for any wicked problem] determines the nature of the problem's resolution' (Rittel and Webber, 1973: 166). However, singular choices often lead to incremental actions – working on part of the problem or addressing only symptoms. It is important to track and examine the multiple pathways along which the current housing situation in England has been reached – and therefore show how different paths are connected and how past planning and housing policy interventions evidence different explanations for selectively observed stresses. The exploration of pathways contrasts system-level response with incremental action.

(10) Finally, while the scientist can hypothesise and test with impunity, planners – or proponents of some other public policy or regulatory/deregulatory response – who work with open systems are 'caught up in the ambiguity of their causal webs' (Rittel and

Webber, 1973: 167). Being wrong is hugely problematic given the effect that mistakes have on people's lives (and the interests that may be offended). Incrementalism serves a purpose – gingerly probing boundaries and promoting small changes. The final feature of wicked problems catalogued by Rittel and Webber is that 'the planner has no right to be wrong' (p. 166). This claim needs some adjustment for the English context: it is politicians who are fearful of experimentation, who will move slowly, take tentative steps and prioritise the interests of their core constituencies. These are not only parliamentary or ward constituency interests, but also powerful corporate interests: landowners and the national and international investors who support the construction and housebuilding industries.

Investors have become particularly important as financial markets have matured and new pathways for capital investment into housing have opened up. London's housing market is truly global – an engine of growth, spending and broader market support (Rossall Valentine, 2015; Atkinson et al, 2016a; Wallace et al, 2017). Rittel and Webber (1973: 167) declared that 'the industrial age greatly expanded cultural diversity. Post-industrial society is likely to be far more differentiated than any in all of past history'. Their point was that once homogenous social interests had splintered between competing publics. Social pluralism had become the norm – generating sub-politics and triggering the pursuit of multiple and frequently incompatible goals (p. 168). The housing crisis exists in a context of socioeconomic pluralism, a diverse political economy and ecosystem of actors and powerful interests, whom planners and politicians must work with in pursuit of their own objectives: (a) support for a housing market in which prices rise but remain affordable relative to earnings; and (b) support for a development sector that builds homes where and when they are needed, but not in locations where they might disrupt either amenity or existing property values. 'Getting it wrong' means failing to achieve (a) and (b) or allowing these objectives to conflict.

It is the *assetisation* of housing that leaves governments with little room for manoeuvre, as sustained growth in asset value is the principal measure of success in housing policy, at many different levels and for many different actors. But across the wider ecosystem, households unable to get on, or stay on, this economic treadmill are looking for alternative ways of meeting their own housing needs. There is a rekindled interest in self-build housing (Benson and Hamiduddin, 2017), co-housing (Tummers, 2016) and other forms of community-led provision (Field and Layard, 2017) that find ways to step outside usual market processes. But, and despite some local success stories, all such alternatives struggle to impact on the broader crisis of housing access given the particular property and market orthodoxies with which they must compete. Hope for some resolution to this crisis seems to lie in a re-evaluation of what 'getting it wrong' looks like: a falling number of households able to buy their own home and an increasing number spending long periods in an expensive and unstable private rented sector. Perhaps politicians have already exercised their right to get it wrong and a chance now exists to do more than gingerly probe the boundaries of the existing system.

Moving forward

The housing cost and access crisis is patently a wicked problem, incredibly difficult to decode and framed by an economic and political context in which there are many competing interests ready to resist interventions that threaten the status quo. The purpose of presenting housing access as a wicked problem in this chapter has been to scotch the idea that simple solutions or single levers can deliver a new accommodation in which welfare is optimised and there is lasting resolution of the crisis. Housing is a wicked problem because:

1. There is no definitive or single formulation of why current stresses have arisen. Different formulations of the problem compete with one another. They often share components, but varying weight is attached to particular drivers – to patterns of land ownership, planning processes, the behaviours and interests of different actors, to capital investment, to the role of the state (versus the role of the market) in producing housing, to patterns of exchange and consumption of housing relative to other assets and so forth. Pathways are seen as more or less important, as dominant or subservient, depending on the world view of the observer.

2. Interventions in an open system will have complex knock-on effects. Rittel and Webber (1973) articulated this as there being no 'stopping rule' for wicked problems. Interventions in the housing system, whatever form they take, will have lasting economic and environmental impacts – new challenges to address and resolve.

3. The judgement as to whether one intervention is better than another – and whether outcomes are 'good' or 'bad' – appears to depend, for housing, on market position and interest. One set of interests appears to be served by housing scarcity and

asset-value growth. Some of those left behind can be assisted into homeownership by a variety of government schemes and interventions. That assistance provides further *market support*, which households/investors nearer the top of the housing pyramid will be happy to pay for: tax investment will be returned through sustained rental income and asset appreciation. Only the most vulnerable households miss out, but poverty – and the 'gap between rich and poor' – is in any case inevitable in conservative thinking (Dorey, 2011: 49). Yet to sustain this system, ordinary households need to take on and service ever more debt, introducing an instability that is accentuated by reduced investment in productive sectors, overreliance on 'nominal growth' (Christophers, 2010), and risk to earnings. What we have is bad, and there are opportunities to build consensus around alternatives.

4. Given the shock – and 'waves of repercussions' – that big shifts in the treatment of housing could generate, and the difficulty of foreseeing and mitigating knock-on effects, a focus on 'curing symptoms' may appear sensible. For housing in England, this means spending Housing Benefit on short-term accommodation for some of the most vulnerable individuals and households and a preference for tacit land-use planning interventions – requiring affordable housing as a price for development permission – that do not impinge upon, or disrupt, the underlying mode of production. These are merely a price to be paid for the preservation of a status quo, and they help circumvent the risks – including the political risks – of more radical action.

5. Indeed, radical experimentation is difficult, although nowadays complex modelling of fiscal and other forms of intervention in the housing system is possible. But modelling seldom reveals all the impacts and risks associated with real-world intervention. Past interventions through different areas of housing, planning and fiscal policy have left traces in inherited housing outcomes; lives have been 'irreversibly influenced' – people today, for example, enduring poor-quality rented housing might, a generation ago, have had access to better-quality council homes. Housing access is a wicked problem because experimentation is difficult and interventions have deep and lasting impacts on people's lives.

6. Because there is no definitive formulation of the housing problem – but rather many permutations of causes – a vast array

of interventions are possible. Judgement always plays a big part in determining action, alongside political reality. Interventions are always partial, addressing not only the symptoms but also the needs of different political constituencies. This is clear from the history of planning and housing policy in England and its targeted focus on the needs of different groups and interests.

7. The housing crisis is a product of its context: its rootedness in systems of property, finance, economics, social welfare, environmental priority and political ambition. This makes it essentially unique, meaning that while inspiration might be sought from remedies applied elsewhere (in other contexts), those remedies are unlikely to be transportable. It is useful to take inspiration from alternative patterns of land ownership, systems of property/land tax, planning systems or welfare models. But how they might work in *this* political economy (of regulation and of governance and economic processes), and what broader implications might follow from structural adjustment, needs to be carefully considered. Interventions that acknowledge the uniqueness of context are needed.

8. The crisis of housing access and affordability is also a symptom of another problem – or is embedded in an economic context that has become reliant on housing as a financial asset. This is a 'high-level' problem, which is potentially difficult to address. But acting incrementally, at a lower level, has the implicit objective of 'marginal improvement' (creating access opportunities or easing affordability barriers for specific groups in particular places), and 'marginal improvement does not guarantee overall improvement' (Rittel and Webber, 1973: 165).

9. However, the idea of the housing crisis being embedded in a changed economic situation, in which nominal growth is extracted from assets and the vitality of an economy is measured in the rising aggregate value of those assets ('asset-sheet growth'), is not universally accepted to be its prime driver. This wicked problem has been explained in numerous, and often more prosaic, ways. Those explanations are parallel pathways, all leading to the same destination. Acceptance of a single cause would surely result in support for a single solution. But declining housing affordability/ access, like other wicked problems, is a socioeconomic outcome with mixed and contested causes. Multiple pathways have been

traced, privileged by some and dismissed by others. These pathways often evidence the changing function of housing and governments' shifting treatment of housing as a social good, to be bureaucratically and directly allocated, or a market outcome, to be indirectly facilitated.

10. In our system of parliamentary democracy and in the context of an unbalanced and underperforming economy, politicians are fearful of interventions in the housing system that could potentially threaten growth or offend business interests. Bold interventions are difficult; moreover, there is a preference for 'smoke and mirrors' – actions that appear to broaden housing access but also support market growth; and that simultaneously speak to different constituencies. It was noted earlier in this chapter that *help to buy* and stamp duty exclusions bring marginal access benefits in the short term but are more fundamentally about supporting house prices over a longer period. What are the parameters of success in housing policy and what does 'getting it wrong' look like? If the priority is market support then the unbroken rise in house prices would seem to be a good outcome, only tarnished by widening access inequality, rising household debt and sluggish consumer spending. The emphasis on rising prices as a marker of success has flattered the housing system, given the stresses and inequities that this emphasis has generated. Politicians have already exercised their right to get it wrong, but it is only as the full nature of economic linkages are revealed, and vulnerabilities exposed, that we can say that the economic growth achieved on the back of housing – being unequal and unstable – has not compensated for the great many negative social outcomes.

Seven of these ten characteristics can, I think, be generally accepted and little more needs to be said. But three require further attention for the following reasons. First, broad economic linkages – between *assets and homes in a changing economy* – need to be exposed if we are to reveal the 'higher level' of the housing crisis (mainly the eighth proposition, but linking to others). Second, by reviewing different formulations or the pathways to crisis, it will be possible to reveal the opportunities that exist for reversal or new actions in specific domains – including tax policy and land-use planning – (mainly the ninth proposition but linking also to the first). And third, there is a pressing need to understand the challenge of building consensus – the possibility of moving to a 'good' solution for the majority by showing that the housing crisis is socially and economically pervasive. Very few actors occupy exclusively 'good' market positions: asset-based growth, underpinned by debt and weak productivity, presents risk to all (mainly the third proposition). The next three chapters focus on these concerns, beginning with the broader economic context and crisis, of which housing access and affordability is a symptom.

3

Housing's economic context

This chapter is concerned with the wider economic canvas introduced in the first two chapters and with the transformation of homes into assets – a focus for investment and a source of income and capital appreciation. The housing crisis is situated in this canvas, and more specifically in the changing profile of the economy and a *capital switch* into fixed assets (facilitated by the maturation of capital markets and by the various tools of financialisation). There are three crucial narratives here. The first concerns broader economic change and how the UK economy, in the postwar period, became unbalanced – 'away from business investment and exports' (Osborne, 2014). The second narrative is the movement of capital into land, property and property-related financial products – a mix of 'direct' and 'indirect' investment, which risks depriving the wider economy of active capital (business) investment. The third and final narrative concerns the UK's reliance on public revenues (tax take) from investment in fixed assets – commercial and residential property – derived from general property and transaction taxes, which rise with property values and therefore infer clear 'public' interest in keeping house prices on an upward track (tax dependence on rising land and property prices is different from the benefits other countries derive from control over land and land rent). These narratives begin at separate points but eventually come together, interacting to shift the function of housing, producing economic volatility, centred on the wider investment market, alongside a dependence on rising house prices.

The chapter is divided into four parts. These are concerned with, first, the UK's shifting economic profile over the last 50 years and investment flows; second, processes behind the switch of capital into fixed assets, and with financialisation – the shift to profit-making through financial channels 'rather than through trade and commodity production' (Krippner, 2005: 181; see also Arrighi, 1994); third, with sources of tax revenue and the argument that there is public interest in rising house prices; and fourth, with the interaction of these shifts and their responsibility for critical tensions, and injustices (Rolnik, 2013) in the housing market.

However, before embarking on this journey, one further point needs to be made concerning housing's role in national economies, often as an instrument of economic development. The centrality of housebuilding to a network of *productive* industries is captured in the following quote by Lord Beaverbrook in the 1930s, in an interview with a US newspaper:

> Things are going well in this country. The government is strong and the country is recovering. What is the reason? House-building. Just that. The burst of activity in the house-building industry lies at the back of the whole of this welcome wave of recovery. No form of expenditure spreads its effects so quickly through every branch of industry as house-building. None touches the whole economic structure in the same way. It is not only a question of a boom in the brick business or cement. There are also electric appliances of every kind, electric wire (with a reaction in the copper market), paint, timber, wallpaper, nails, slates, and so forth. Then when you put the roof on and get the new tenants in, there is furniture to be got. Don't imagine they bring old furniture. They do not. And the further out of town you build these houses the better it is. For then the tenants must buy a motor-car if they do not already have one. It is my belief that you would do well in America too, if you embarked on a big housing programme instead of squandering your money on other and less fruitless directions. (Parliamentary Archives BBK/L/61; quoted in Stirling, 2019: no page number)

Housebuilding retains this productive economic function and much of Lord Beaverbrook's thinking (with the exception, perhaps, of promoting increased car-dependence) would be familiar to today's policy makers and economic commentators. Analysis in this chapter, however, draws attention to an important shift in housing's economic function: while housebuilding continues to support other industries (hence the case for more of it, even where it is not the route to greater affordability), the assetisation of privately owned housing (Beaverbrook's focus was public investment in council housing) has given housing a distinctly different role within national economies and personal finance. The foundations for this shift were laid in the 1960s: the removal of 'Schedule A' tax in the Finance Act 1963 meant that homeowners were no longer taxed on the 'imputed rent' of owning their own homes, and they were likewise exempted from Capital Gains Tax when it was created in the Finance Act 1965. Schedule A tax had previously been levied (and paid under a general income tax code) from owner-occupiers. Margaret Thatcher, in an article for the *Finchley Press*, explained to her constituents that:

> If land is let, the owner is paid rent; if however the owner chooses to occupy the land or house himself, he is enjoying in kind the rent he would otherwise receive in cash. He is therefore deemed to have an income from the ownership of his house equal to the rent forgone. The amount of this notional income is called the 'annual value', sometimes referred to as the 'gross annual value'. It is defined as the rent at which the property is worth to be let by the year, on the conventional tenancy conditions. (Thatcher, 1960)

She went on to offer advice on allowances that could be claimed against Schedule A. Return to a similar system today – as part of a 'land value tax' – is viewed as a way to more fairly apportion tax liability to those who hold significant land and property assets. Its removal made holding these assets, as an owner-occupier, more attractive. Early acknowledgement of housing's 'asset function', just a few years after the abolition of the Schedule A charge on owner-occupiers, can be found in the 1971 Housing White Paper: 'if the householder buys his house on a mortgage, he builds up by steady saving a *capital asset* for himself and his dependents' (Para. 4).

As noted before, holding housing as asset is not only the preserve of owner-occupiers. Personal mortgage borrowing and finance for owner-occupation is just one investment path; likewise, the accumulation of equity in a single, owner-occupied, home (and releasing equity or earning interest on mortgage lending) are the simplest forms of profit-taking. Changes in these basic practices – more borrowing and borrowing to support investment – are surface processes that have underlying drivers. Beneath this surface, housing has been transformed from being a support for the productive economy (linking from construction to many commodity sectors) to being central to a financial-service economy, as debt, rather than construction and other productive activities, became more central to national wealth creation, measured in gross domestic product (GDP). The financialisation described by Krippner (2005) played a big part in this, with various episodes of reregulation – including controls on lending (see Chapter 4) and capital controls (see later discussion in this chapter) – facilitating the movement of greater volumes of money, derived from capital markets, into housing consumption.

The changing profile of the UK economy

In his Mansion House speech, as well as noting the apparently irreconcilable tensions within Britain's housing market, George Osborne (2014) also drew attention to Britain's successes as a provider of financial services: "Our financial exports grew 10% last year, and our surplus in finance and insurance has reached £45 billion – twice as much as our closest competitors." An expansive account of those successes – including Britain being the headquarters for "some of the world's largest insurance firms", "two thirds of all Renminbi payments outside of China and Hong Kong now [taking] place in London", and "Britain [being] not just the Western hub of Chinese finance – but of Islamic finance too" – was prefaced with an admission that "at home, our economy is still too unbalanced, so I am the first to say we need to continue our efforts to *boost business investment*, exports and housing supply". Reading through the speech, the imbalance relates to success in financial services on the global stage versus a relative lack of investment in traditional business, which translates into weak manufacturing growth and a trade deficit in (non-financial) goods. An increase in housing supply (combined with intervention in levels of mortgage lending) is part of how "we stop rising house prices leading to an unsustainable rise in household indebtedness, and threatening the wider economy".

The inference is that households chase those rising prices and, in doing so, become unsustainably indebted, which in turn, causes consumer spending to stall. The lending of 'fictional capital' is part of this (as banks pursue profit through the distribution of debt) but the main response – Osborne's 'third pillar', next to market supports and the protection of financial stability through bank regulation – is to see "a lot more homes being built in Britain". These homes are seen as part of the answer to both the housing crisis and the risk of economic instability arising from indebtedness, although that indebtedness underpins the growth in financial income. The first section of this chapter is primarily concerned with the imbalance between growth in the financial sector (and in profit-taking through financial channels) and the squeezed space of commodity production. What does the imbalance look like and what has been the role of housing in shifting economic activity to the service sector?

An unbalanced economy

In broad terms, the changing economic profile (and hence 'balance') of the United Kingdom (the level at which most data focus) can be read in contributions made to GDP by different sectors and industries. Total GDP for the UK (chained volume measure) was £493,278 million in the first quarter of 2018 (ONS, 2018b, *Gross Domestic Product*). Presently, the service sector contributes roughly 80% of GDP across four service types: distribution, hotels and restaurants (17.3%); transport, storage and communication (13.2%); business services and finance (41.5%); and government and other services (28%). (These figures are percentage of services from the February 2018 release of the *Index of Services*; ONS, 2018c.) The remaining 20% of GDP is divided between production (14%), construction (6%) and agriculture (1%). Figures from ONS (its March 2018 release of the *Index of Production*; ONS, 2018d) show that the production component of the economy is dominated by manufacturing (72%), with remaining production comprising mining and quarrying; electricity; gas; steam and air conditioning; and water supply, sewerage and waste management. There are no subdivisions in the agriculture component. The construction sector is similarly aggregated, though it is possible to discern patterns of activity from a range of data sets. 'New order' figures, for example, show that 30% of activity comprised 'new housing' in 2016, of a total new order value of £66,126 million. ONS points out that not all new orders become 'output', so the total here will not match the total value of construction output.

These figures indicate the overall shape of the economy – the contributions from different sectors – and clearly reveal the imbalance towards the service sector. It is of course well known that the UK's economy is structured in this way and that 'financial services' are a very significant component of a very large service sector, delivering a trade surplus in finance and insurance. Tracking changes over time requires the use of consistent data. ONS provide useful indexed data on GDP growth by sector: quarter on quarter growth using chained volume measures (CVM) show services on a steady upward track since the GFC. Other sectors, especially construction, display greater volatility and track well below the service sector. However, quarter on quarter growth figures are concerned with performance of sectors relative to an index point. Staying with the issue of 'balance' across sectors, aggregated time-series data have been analysed by Rhodes (2016) who uses the 2007 Standard Industrial Classification (SIC) to show simplified trends over time. Usefully, Rhodes pulls manufacturing from the production component and retains services as an aggregated sector. In line with the index of services figures presented above, he notes the 80%, 10% and 6% split between services, manufacturing and construction (ignoring the remaining 4%, which comprises other production and agriculture) (Rhodes, 2016: 3). These components contributed £1.3 trillion, £162 billion and £102 billion respectively to UK economic output in 2015. The service sector component had contributed 69% of output in 1990 and the manufacturing sector 18%. Services then grew as manufacturing shrank. Because of changes to the SIC, Rhodes offers two sets of time-series data: one covering the period 1970 to 2010 and another from 1990 to 2015. The longer-run data reveal the broad shift from manufacturing to services and also the rise of business services and the finance industry (see Figures 3.1 and 3.2).

During the 40-year period depicted in Figures 3.1 and 3.2, the gross value added (GVA is the contribution of parts of the economy, less costs incurred) *at 2010 prices* from the service sector rose from £279.5 billion to £1,008.1 billion. Business services and the finance industry contribution grew from £81.7 billion to £439.5 billion. The overall contribution of that component to total economic output was 33%, or 43.2% of the total services sector (which roughly equates to the 2018 Index of Services figure of 41.5%). The total services figure for 2010 stood at 77%. Switching now to the shorter-run data (1990 to 2015), the total services percentage jumps up to 80% but the SIC changes mean that service subcomponents are different. Finance and insurance have been separated out and real

Figure 3.1: Services vs manufacturing – percentage of total economic output, GVA, SIC2003

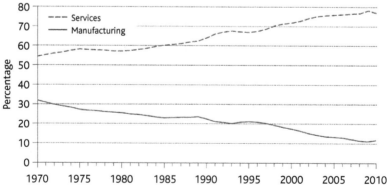

Source: ONS, from Rhodes, 2016: 15

estate is in a category on its own. Likewise, professional and support is also separate but government, health education and defence have been brought together. These complications mean that the longer-run data provide a broader view of significant changes (depicted in Figures 3.1 and 3.2) but the shorter-run offer more detailed insights into the growth of subcomponents linked to property. Between 1990 and 2015, professional and support service industries (legal, accountancy, scientific, architectural and consultancy services) grew by 190% (£137 billion) in real terms (Rhodes, 2016: 6). Similarly, real estate (that is, activities related to the sales, rent or management of commercial or residential properties) grew by 91% (£95 billion) (Rhodes, 2016: 6) (see Figure 3.3).

The real estate subcomponent on its own (at £215 billion in 2015) is a bigger contributor to economic output than manufacturing (£162 billion), construction (£102 billion), finance and insurance (£120 billion) or professional and support services (£205 billion). However, in aggregate, subcomponents relating to finance, construction, sales and leasing of property (that is, the finance, production and consumption of physical assets) are implicated in about a third of total economic output. Assuming a proportion of manufacturing (and also mining and extractives) serve the property sector, alongside government services, then the total GVA contribution relating to the built environment is likely to be closer to half of total economic output. These data, however, do not reveal the split between commercial and residential property or say anything about the total value of housing production and consumption (the latter including sales, renting and related finance). They provide just a general account

Figure 3.2: Business services and finance industry vs manufacturing – percentage of total economic output, GVA, SIC2003

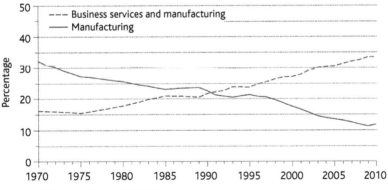

Source: ONS, from Rhodes, 2016: 15

Figure 3.3: Economic output as a percentage of the UK total – manufacturing vs real estate

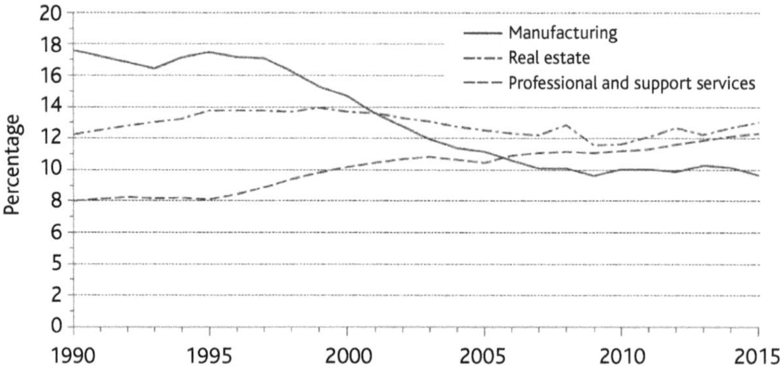

Source: ONS, Rhodes, 2016: 7

of economic change, hinting at the enlarged role of property in setting the UK's economic trajectory. Others have drawn attention to increased economic reliance on finance and services supporting the consumption of fixed assets (or trading in financial products that are backed by those assets), observing this trend not only in the UK but across a number of countries. Housing has been a particular focus for many commentators. As part of its 'housing and the economy' focus, for example, the UK Collaborative Centre for Housing Evidence has started to map the extensive literature on housing taxation in Organisation for Economic Co-operation and Development (OECD) countries. Its premise is that:

> The rise of housing as an asset class, including for owner occupiers, raises many social and policy relevant questions, including those related to housing taxation. If tax-advantaging housing leads to the under-accumulation of productive capital, then this may have an important impact on UK productivity performance [and] also on the efficiency of housing markets and the state of public finance. (Soaita, 2018: 2)

There will also be implications for resource allocation (between owners and non-owners) and for 'progressivity and inequality' (Soaita, 2018: 2). Increased volumes of capital moving into housing result in both the economic imbalance observed in high-level data (including the data presented in this chapter) and the social stresses described elsewhere in this book: an unequal distribution of housing resource as access is impeded by price rises, driven by loan credit (and broader investment flows) and outpacing workplace earnings.

The economic imbalance argument, linked to a diversion of investment away from productive sectors, is not new. In the early 1980s, the further promotion of owner-occupation through the *right to buy* (on top of the more general tax changes noted earlier) was expected to impact on the ability of building societies to lend to business. This was the view of the Royal Town Planning Institute (RTPI):

> The Institute is concerned about the way in which [*right to buy*] sales will divert investment from other areas and sectors. The wider aspect of this is that owner-occupation is, in itself, a vast consumer of investment resources and any significant acceleration of the trend to owner-occupation inevitably diverts more money into unproductive investment and away from other sectors where it is needed. (Parliamentary Archives 7398/7440; quoted in Stirling, 2019: no page number)

Can this diversion of investment be discerned from available data? Can the broader patterns of sectoral economic shift noted above therefore be squared, at least generally, with the raising of finance from banks and capital markets? To what extent are UK banks prioritising lending on fixed assets and therefore driving the broad economic shifts outlined above?

Patterns of lending to industries and households

The Bank of England provides short-run data, typically for the last five to ten years. General data are available on money and credit growth (M4 and M4 lending), lending to households, and lending to businesses (divided between construction; transport, storage and communication; real estate, professional services and support activities; and manufacturing) by banks and the net finance raised by those sectors from banks, building societies and from capital markets. Short-run data, however, suggest significant monthly variation and no clear trends. Since the GFC, the monthly growth in net finance raised by all non-financial industries has slowed, though manufacturing is currently outperforming both construction and real estate (Bank of England, 2018, *Lending to Industries – Headline Flows*) in terms of finance raised (in the last 18 months). Usefully, the New Economics Foundation

(NEF) examines longer-run data and compares 'credit stock' (loans outstanding) as a percentage of GDP for all non-financial firms against that of financial corporations, as well as credit stock in domestic mortgages and general consumer credit. Using Bank of England data, the NEF is able to show that the credit stock in housing (channelled through domestic mortgages) has, at least since 1990, far exceeded that in non-financial firms, including manufacturing (see Figure 3.4). Ryan-Collins et al (2017: 117) track these data back further, to 1963. At that time, domestic mortgages already accounted for almost twice as much lending as loans issued to non-financial corporations (roughly 17% of GDP compared to 9%). That ratio remained largely unchanged until 1980. Lending to both sectors spiked in the early 1970s (in September 1971, the Bank of England cut direct controls on lending through amendment to its Competition and Credit Control Policy – see Chapter 4) before settling back. Ryan-Collins et al reflect on the pattern of change over the last 40 years:

> Since the early 1980s, UK banks have significantly increased their lending to domestic mortgages relative to GDP. Domestic mortgage lending has expanded from 20% of GDP in the early 1980s to over 60% now, while lending to non-finance firms has stayed between 20% and 30% of GDP. (Ryan-Collins et al, 2017: 118)

Figure 3.4: Nominal credit stocks as a percentage of GDP

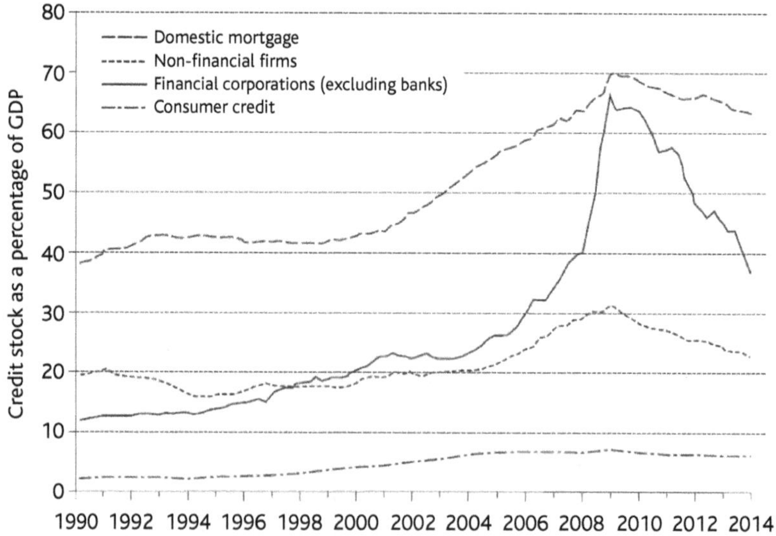

Source: New Economics Foundation, 2016

The shift into residential mortgages is only part of the story. Data from the ONS point to a broader turn away from manufacturing, as a GVA contributor, towards a services-dominated economy. While focused on land-related credit, Ryan-Collins et al also examine sectoral lending by UK banks over time. Between 1986 and 2014, lending to non-financial corporations (excluding real estate) faced a continual squeeze – from more than half of all bank lending at the beginning of the period to less than 10% at the end. If commercial real estate is included in lending to non-financial corporations, its share of finance rose from 14% to 60% over the same period. Another constituent of non-financial corporations – estate agents and real estate intermediaries – saw their borrowing as a proportion of GDP rise from 1.5% to 11% at the eve of the GFC, before falling back to 7% (Ryan-Collins et al, 2017: 119).

Patterns of lending square with the observation of an 'imbalance' in the UK economy. It was concluded earlier that 'the total GVA contribution relating to the built environment is likely to be [close] to half of total economic output'. Ryan-Collins et al show that 'land related lending (*excluding construction*) made up 80% of GDP at the height of the financial crisis. It has since reduced to 70%; in 1986, it was just 30%' (2017: 119). Data on GVA contribution and bank lending by industry sector are not entirely compatible. Services, for example, are distributed between non-financial and financial firms. Manufacturing is only part of the non-financial sector, which includes real estate intermediaries in the lending data. In the GVA data, these are found in a real estate component that cannot be split between commercial and domestic real estate. What we have here is two broad pictures – on sectoral contributions to economic output and bank lending by industry sector – which appear to connect: more capital flowing into particular sectors – real estate and related services – enlarges their contribution to the national economy and leaves less capital investment for other sectors, squeezing the contribution, for example, of 'production' and especially manufacturing. In Chapter 4, more attention is given to the impact of these flows on the housing market and on house prices (and the 'inequality' noted by Soaita, 2018: 2) and also to the 'positive feedback cycle' between house prices and mortgage loan credit. That cycle works as follows:

> if mortgage [and commercial real estate] lending outpaces the supply of new domestic and commercial dwellings, this will cause a rise in land prices. As land prices rise, households and firms are forced to take out larger loans to

get on the property ladder, boosting the banks' profits and capital (the money banks must hold to cover defaults). This enables banks to issue more loans which further pushes up prices until such a point that property prices are many times people's incomes. (Ryan-Collins et al, 2017: 119)

The UK 'is not alone in having its banks turn into real estate lenders' (Ryan-Collins et al, 2017: 119) or in reaping the consequences of this investment switch. This is a subject that has attracted considerable attention for a number of decades.

Explaining the capital switch into fixed assets

In 1978, David Harvey pointed to an increased 'urbanisation of capital' into fixed assets, including housing. A summary of this process was presented in Chapter 1, where it was also noted that the maturing of financial markets has increased the number of pathways along which capital can move into and out of land and property, accelerating the accumulation of capital (and not only 'surplus' capital) into the built environment and giving that accumulation greater permanence. Harvey's 'primary circuit', along which profit-seeking capital flows, is industrial production, with investment in that circuit generating capital return. However, the capacity of that circuit to deliver profit is fixed (or linked to the size of commodity markets): increasing investment above a particular level will not increase returns as consumer markets cannot, *ad infinitum*, absorb more goods. Indeed, capital movements into productive activities risk lower returns as markets are saturated and the prices of goods fall. Capital switch before that point is reached means redirecting surplus capital into long-term *fixed* assets, which provide a place to store wealth and generate further income by capturing land rents. This becomes a 'secondary circuit' and, as Gotham (2009) observes, a source of further capital accumulation that may do more than act as a temporary sink for surplus capital. The circuit is sustained by money supply and by banking systems that, because of various episodes of deregulation, have favoured the issuing of loans on property and the land on which it sits (Harvey, 1978) over riskier investment in productive activities. The role of financial institutions in supporting the capital switch described by Harvey and by others, and also their role in creating new ways of extracting financial income from fixed assets, has today been presented as financialisation: a growth in financial actors and tools linked to the secondary circuit that have spearheaded the structural transformation of many modern economies

(Gotham, 2009; Fernandez and Aalbers, 2016) – including the UK's. One of the key features of financialisation is its embeddedness in a global system of finance and capital movement, which has replaced the challenge of 'spatial fixity' (see Gotham, 2009) with a level of liquidity hitherto associated with non-fixed assets. Financialisation is both a facilitator and accelerator of Harvey's capital switch.

In the 40 years since Harvey's observations, a great many other studies have examined and critiqued the political economy of this 'capital switch'. Effort has been expended on verifying the switch in different parts of the world, starting with the US. Beauregard (1994) examined 'construction investment' during the building boom of 1982 to 1986. His focus was mainly on capital flowing into construction and, although he found no evidence of relative depletion of investment in industrial production during that period, Beauregard observed how 'real estate investors did heighten significantly the turnover in ownership of existing buildings *relative* to investment in new construction' (1994: 729). Physical expansion of the 'consumption fund' was not at the expense of productive investment in the primary circuit, but that expansion was itself outpaced by investment and transactions in the existing fund, leading Beauregard to conclude that the 'disengagement of capital investment from materially based rhythms of construction activity appears to be a more apt description' of the investment flows observed during the boom (p. 729). This conclusion is linked to Harvey's later observation that 'the financial system has achieved a degree of autonomy from real production unprecedented in capitalism's history' (Harvey, 1989: 194; cited in Beauregard, 1994: 719).

Building on this, an important point emerging from Beauregard's analysis relates to the increasing autonomy of finance capital. It is that autonomy (realised through new investment options and pathways) that provides opportunities for capital switch, opening up the secondary circuit to more than just surplus capital. The circuit is not merely a 'safety valve' (Beauregard, 1994: 729) but an increasingly financialised investment outlet. Whether capital moves into it – or heads to 'stock speculation, overseas markets, government bonds, or the tertiary sector' – will depend on the part played by 'financial intermediaries and … the political and social determinants of the demand for buildings, structures and land forms' (p. 729). Harvey regularly alluded to these actors and forces, and to the shaping of financial markets (Harvey, 1978, 1985). And although Beauregard found it difficult to support Harvey's capital switch thesis – conceding instead that growth in the primary circuit *may* have been less than it might otherwise have been during the boom (because of diversion of investment to the secondary circuit) or that the switch was 'clouded by the infusion of foreign investment capital' – he nevertheless acknowledged the dangers of 'disengagement of real-estate loan activity by large commercial banks from a demand-induced base':

> The buying and selling of properties in order to exploit favourable tax laws or rapidly escalating markets feed a rise in property values that encourages further speculative activity. To this extent, much of the exchange value of the built environment becomes increasingly fictitious and use values become increasingly peripheral … All of this means that city building is less and less responsive to human need and more and more driven by entrepreneurial fervour. (Beauregard, 1994: 730)

In this situation, there is little or no 'consideration of … the contribution of such investments to the development of society'. Much of Beauregard's analysis – and of course Harvey's before – can be seen as a precursor to the more recent focus on the financialisation of the built environment and housing therein. He drew attention to the 'complex financing schemes' that sit behind investments and which 'dissolve immediately after the "deal" into a maze of international financial networks' (1994: 730).

More recent literature on financialisation has responded to Beauregard's claim that capital switch is 'under-theorised' in respect of the role of financial intermediaries and 'political and social determinants'. Gotham, for example, draws attention to the ways in which 'institutional developments' have 'delocalised' residential and commercial property and embedded 'real estate financing within global capital markets' (2006: 231). National governments, he argues, play a critical role in 'creating the institutional conditions and legal mechanisms to transform real estate into a liquid financial asset that is abstracted from local conditions' (p. 233). His specific concern is with the ways in which government-sponsored enterprises in the US have developed a global investor base to finance housing, often by encouraging the growth of REITs or through increased activity in the secondary mortgage market. More generally, he seeks to show how the state's capacity to 'create and control liquid resources [from otherwise illiquid assets] is a powerful mechanism of globalisation' (p. 237). This is achieved, in part, by examining 'regulative and legal infrastructure' and also institutions: that is, 'rules of exchange, governance structures, property rights, and conceptions of control that regularize patterns of real estate activity' (p. 240).

Gotham notes the different dates at which various countries opened their financial markets to foreign participation, liberalising cross-border trade. This happened in the UK in 1979. The end of 'capital controls' was then followed by a 'stretching of real estate activities across borders' as markets opened up to foreign firms. Foreign direct investment in US real estate, for example, rose rapidly – the ratio of real estate foreign direct investment (FDI) to real estate GDP went from 0.44:1 in 1973 to 4.45:1 in 2000, and overseas investment by US firms increased from roughly $1 billion in 1982 to $6 billion in 2003 (constant 2003 dollars). The issuing of mortgage-backed securities by government-sponsored enterprises in a 'secondary mortgage market' was said by Gotham to have had a 'catalytic' role in the growth of 'global financial markets and networks of housing finance'. The primary mortgage market is where homebuyers secure loans from banks for home purchase. The secondary mortgage market exists to increase market liquidity and draw investors into housing finance. In the US, the Federal National Mortgage Association (FNMA – known as Fannie Mae) and the Federal Home Loan Mortgage Company (FHLMC – known as Freddie Mac) purchase mortgages from the originating banks, repackage them as mortgage-backed or 'debt' securities and sell to institutional investors. In this way, 'illiquid financial assets' become 'liquid capital market securities' (Gotham, 2006: 257): one third of outstanding US mortgage debt was securitised in this way in 1988 and nearly two thirds by the late 1990s.

In short, Gotham illustrates how capital is switched into the secondary circuit through the creation of a market for 'originator' mortgages. This is not achieved through deregulation but rather through 'legislation and policies that have promoted the growth of securitisation' (Gotham, 2006: 268) and other instruments of financialisation, including REITs. These infrastructures and institutional environments generate their own demand for primary market mortgage lending (and credit supply), which becomes a means of raising finance through the sale of debt to investors. The extension of (ever bigger) loans on property is motivated by investor appetite for securities, not demand for homes: this is Beauregard's 'disengagement of real-estate loan activity by large commercial banks from a demand-induced base' (1994: 730). Gotham offers his own warning as to the potential consequences of this shift, suggesting that it will increasingly tie local impact to global-level developments in financial markets and exacerbate regional imbalances as investment, rather than utility, drives the demand for property and land.

The equivalent infrastructures and institutions in the UK are examined by Wainwright (2009), who looks at the development of residential mortgage-backed securities (RMBS) in the US and their transfer to the UK banking system. Securities offer a fast income stream for lenders and facilitate the shifting of higher-risk mortgages from lenders' balance sheets to investors (Wainwright, 2009: 374). They are structured in complicated ways and packaged and delivered by special delivery vehicles and by investment banks, which provide this type of structured finance (see Wainwright, 2009, 374–5). In the US, the creation of a secondary mortgage market was facilitated by the federal government, through the creation of Fannie Mae and Freddie Mac, as a means of transferring an element of risk away from homebuyers and thereby expanding homeownership (Gotham, 2006: 257). In the UK, government played no direct part in establishing a secondary mortgage market; rather, financial institutions (at home and abroad) grasped the opportunities presented by the 'reregulation' of the UK's financial markets in 1986 (Wainwright, 2009: 377).

In that year, the Financial Services Act opened the mortgage market to new financial institutions, including banks. Previously, only building societies could offer mortgages. The Building Societies Act of the same year allowed building societies to become banks. Wainwright points to two important implications of this reregulation: US investment banks could establish mortgage-issuing subsidiaries in the UK, 'while retail banks, which would later become the largest securitisers in the UK, began originating mortgages' (Wainwright, 2009: 377). Thereafter, 'the concept [of securitisation] travelled relatively freely from the US to the UK in the 1980s, as American investment banks – experienced in performing securitization – began to promote securitization to UK lenders' (p. 378). Through the 1980s and into the 1990s, however, the investment banks struggled to reconcile these complex finance structures with UK law. Eventually, though, after a number of stops and starts, the selling of 'RMBS notes' on international markets gathered pace, stimulating the:

> expansion of UK mortgage lending and the profitability of securitization, which dramatically increased the reliance of the UK mortgage market on the liquidity of RMBS markets and an abundance of low-priced capital obtained through the global capital markets. (Wainwright, 2009: 381)

'As a proportion of GDP, RMBS increased from nearly 2% in 1999 to nearly 27% of GDP by the start of the financial crisis in 2007'

(Milne and Wood, 2014: 26; cited in Ryan-Collins et al, 2017: 139). Creating a secondary mortgage market, linked to global capital markets, increased the UK banking system's vulnerability to the credit crunch of 2007 – not because of direct involvement of UK banks in US subprime RMBS, but because of the 'geographical contagion of risk through the international financial system' (Wainwright, 2009: 382). More generally – and of more direct relevance here – securitisation has increased the flow of credit into housing, with that credit driving up house prices before and after the GFC. This point is also made by Ryan-Collins et al (2017: 139), who argue that the 'large expansion of mortgage credit [seen in the UK] would not have been possible if banks were solely dependent on retail deposits for their funding'. Securitisation supercharges the 'positive feedback cycle' between house prices and mortgage loan credit noted earlier, enabling 'mortgage issuers to offer a wider range of mortgage products at much lower rates of interest and offer them at a much higher loan-to-value (LTV) ratio'. More people can therefore access homeownership but at 'higher price-to-income and mortgage debt-to-income ratios' (Ryan-Collins et al, 2017: 139). Further complications arising from 2007 have included the negative impact on UK pension funds, causing a flight to housing by direct investors, and 'credit rationing', making mortgages inaccessible to borrowers 'with less than a perfect credit history' (Wainwright, 2009: 383), adding to inequalities around housing access.

Like Beauregard (1994), Gotham (2006) and others, Wainwright questions whether it is over-accumulation in the primary circuit that results in capital switch (into the built environment) or whether the secondary circuit is just simply a very attractive investment destination. 'Funding mortgage production is profitable', and it is that profitability, alongside reregulation in the UK and direct government action in the US, that has increased the volume of passive investment in mortgages and, indirectly, in housing. Mortgages (credit) drive prices and also allow prospective homebuyers (with the requisite credit history) to access property that would otherwise be too expensive (credit sustains expensiveness – see Ryan-Collins et al, 2017: 139: home ownership is accessed 'at a higher price-to-income ratio'). Because of the price-setting role of credit, it has been suggested (see, for example, Keen, 2017) that credit rationing, slowly introduced, would calm prices: it would make the stock of existing housing more affordable. However, links through the secondary mortgage market mean that such measures would disrupt the operation of structured finance. Falling prices would likely cause a flight from UK RMBS notes and therefore deprive banks of their income streams, leading to a banking crisis that would affect all sectors of the economy.

It is not easy to disentangle housing and house prices from the complicated web of economic and financial relationships that have developed over time. Housing occupies centre stage in the economic life of the nation, by providing a focus for construction activity and also through the indirect investment in housing linked to the wider operation of the residential mortgage market. Banks are not constituted to support the expansion of homeownership or, more generally, facilitate access to homes. Rather, they are in the business of generating revenue streams through lending. This is achieved through the creation of debt, which is itself supported by the transformation of that debt into tradeable mortgage products. I have focused on this issue here because while direct investment/ trading in property (supported by mortgage lending) would seem to be the more obvious process bidding up prices, it is through the wider financial sector that housing (as the most important and ubiquitous property asset) gains its central position in the wider economic canvas – supporting growth in financial services. Regulation in the housing market which aimed to address spiralling prices (for example, limiting mortgage finance, changing tax rules or 'de-financialising' that market in some way, through restrictions on trading asset-backed financial products) would generate impacts across this web of economic and financial relationships. The substitution of 'growth in the real economy' with growth centred on property, and levered through financial products, also means that there is likely to be little appetite for potentially disruptive change. The economic reality, for many countries, is to extract growth through rent – locally and directly and, in response to spatial fixity, through financial instruments that open up that rent to a wider market of investors. However, for national economies:

> rent does not constitute added value, and simply sitting on property assets – whatever new-fangled financial engineering techniques might be applied to them – does not create value. Any apparent 'economic growth' located in the property rental market must ultimately be grounded in, and sustained by, growth in the real economy of productive activity. If such growth is not occurring, and surplus value is not being generated, the notional growth delivered by the landlord class must eventually come crashing back down to earth. (Christophers, 2010: 106)

The production of housing is part of the real economy of productive activity – housebuilding continues to connect to 'all branches of industry'. The consumption of housing, however, is not a productive activity, but it is an activity on which some economies have become increasingly reliant. In this section, I have reflected on Harvey's broad theorisation of a capital switch into the built environment. This has sometimes proven difficult to detect, but 'new-fangled' financial tools have clearly drawn housing assets into a broader financial sector that is increasingly dependent on the buying and selling of fixed assets, new loans being generated and new means of transforming these otherwise illiquid assets into liquid capital. Beauregard (1994), cited above, drew attention to the way in which these processes led to 'escalating markets [feeding] a rise in property values that encourages further speculative activity' during the US building boom of the 1990s. More recently, Rolnik (2013) has argued that housing itself – like 'pension funds, private equity and hedge funds' – becomes a 'fictitious commodity' when 'taken over by finance', being transformed from a 'sleeping beauty' – an asset owned by traditional means – into a 'fantastic ballet', with assets changing hands through constant and rapid transactions' (Rolnik, 2013: 1058; citing Zivkovic, 2006) both in the real market of physical assets and in the secondary market of related financial products. Rolnik (2013: 1059) claims that this direct commodification of housing, alongside the indirect 'use of housing as an investment asset integrated in a globalized financial market, has profoundly affected the enjoyment of the right to adequate housing across the world'. Citing Schwartz and Seabrooke (2008), she points out that in many Western countries, including the US and the UK, residential mortgage markets represent between 50% and 100% of GDP (Rolnik, 2013: 1059): the actual figure for the UK from 2004 was just over 75%, up from just over 52% in 1992 (Schwartz and Seabrooke, 2008: 249).

These figures are indicative of the level of economic activity centred on housing and the amount of money, supplied by banks, flowing into this form of investment. Prospective homeowners with the right credit histories have often been supported into homeownership, which is, in many parts of the world, 'no longer a goal in itself, but ... a derived goal, a means to an end. Mortgaged homeownership increasingly is there to keep mortgage and financial markets going, rather than being facilitated by those markets' (Aalbers, 2015: 52). Broadly, the apparent social gains or costs of this system are felt by those able or unable to participate in those markets as borrowers. For those unable to participate, either because of credit history or because prices have accelerated beyond their reach, the broader neoliberal project of *substituting* postwar welfare states (Rolnik, 2013: 1060–61) with stored equity in private assets (broadly correlated with the value of the mortgage market relative to GDP, assuming house prices continue to rise) (see Rossi, 2017) mean that non-market housing options are increasingly limited. In the UK, public housing has been transferred into private hands through the *right to buy* as part of a broader economic project that has seen the housing system re-tasked to store, transfer and generate wealth – for individual investors and for the national economy. The wealth generated, however, is notional and not grounded in the added value created by new productive activity (see Christophers, 2010). Watson (2010: 413) argues that the pursuit, and reliance on, the growth of house prices to underpin the total asset value of economies (Christophers' notional growth without added value) is a form of 'house price Keynesianism' of which the UK has become a key proponent. Traditional public housing, let on nominal rather that market-linked rents, has been abandoned in favour of marketised 'affordable housing' that can contribute to this broader economic project.

One fairly simple measure of the growing importance of that project, beyond GDP share in financial services and direct investment in housing, is the amount of tax revenue originating from the housing sector, directly through exchange and transaction and indirectly collected from related financial services and products (rather than directly through land). In short, through taxation, house price Keynesianism and notional growth based on financial services and their real estate component have become an important source of public revenues – as illustrated in the next section.

UK tax revenues

The rising tide of investment in housing and linked mortgage products (directly through construction activity and acquiring and trading in property, and, indirectly through investments in the secondary mortgage market) mean that housing, in general, and the activities of financial intermediaries have become an important source of public revenues in the UK. If real estate is implicated in half of economic growth, and if land and property-related credit accounts for 80% of all lending, then it seems clear that public revenue streams from real estate and the related financial sector will be significant – and critically important in relation to the state's public spending obligations. In 2011, the Office for Budget Responsibility (OBR) provided a special focus on tax revenues from the financial sector, noting that the 'sectoral landscape of the economy' had changed markedly over the previous 30 years. In particular, and confirming the picture presented in this chapter, 'the share of manufacturing in total output [had] fallen while business services and the real estate sectors [had] experienced sharp growth. The financial sector's share of GVA doubled from 2000 to 2008' (OBR, 2011: 89). The size of tax streams from different sectors relates to the profitability of those sectors. On the eve of the GFC, 2007–08, gross trading profits in banking, finance and insurance accounted for around 21% of total profits across all sectors. This meant that the effective tax burden – from income and corporation tax – was highest for financial intermediaries. However:

> The financial crisis then led to revenues from this sector and the related housing sector falling sharply. ... This was one of the primary drivers of the severe deterioration of the UK public finances in recent years, exposing the risks to sustainability of reliance on revenue from these sectors. (OBR, 2011: 89)

As a result, the OBR adopted a more cautious approach to forecasting revenues from the 'financial and housing sectors' after 2011. These were expected to rise out of the 2009–10 trough, but not return to the peak achieved before the GFC (see Figure 3.5).

The financial plus housing line in Figure 3.5 includes capital gains tax, inheritance tax and stamp duty (SDLT). Stamp duty is 'one of the more volatile sources of receipts' (OBR, 2016: 54), bar capital gain tax (also included in Figure 3.5) and revenues from North Sea oil and gas. Volatility arises because 'property transaction taxes involve a very small minority of all potential tax payers each year'. Likewise, there are 'around 28 million dwellings in the UK, but only around 1.2 million residential property transactions each year' (p. 54). Changes in the composition of transactions – alongside the 'large' number of recent policy changes – amplify this volatility, year on year. In 2016–17, stamp duty generated £8.4 billion for HMRC (Scanlon et al, 2017b: 9) and 1.3% of total receipts in the previous year. Because it is a transaction tax, it reduces the number of housing market transactions: it is a tax that many people will pay only if they need to, choosing to extend homes (if they can) rather than moving (unless they must). Its impact on the operation of the housing market, and its culpability, for inefficiencies in that market, are considered in Chapter 4.

Looking broadly at tax receipts from the housing sector, some are clearly 'direct', usually transaction-related – OECD figures show

Figure 3.5: Financial and housing sector receipts

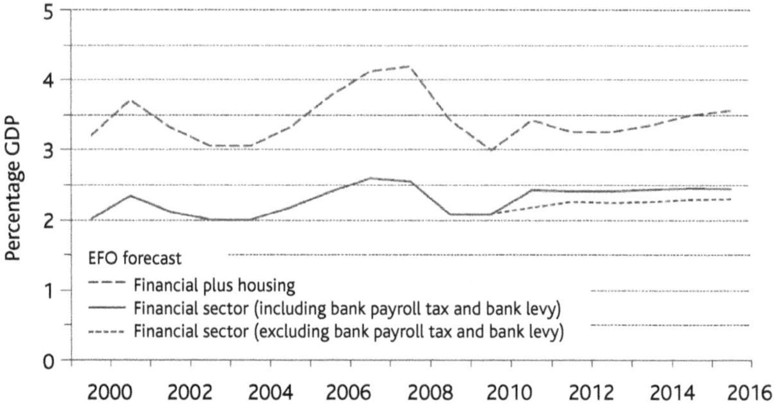

Source: OBR, 2011: 89

that 'property taxes' contribute 13% of public revenues in the UK compared to the OECD average of 6% (OECD, 2017: 2) – while others are indirect and relate to the operation of services and sectors (finance, real estate and construction) that are centred on the financing, production, management and trading of land and property. These indirect taxes are captured as income and corporation taxes and the total proportion relating to residential (as opposed to commercial) property is difficult to size. Income tax accounts for nearly a quarter of all receipts (not including the additional 18% of all receipts received via National Insurance Contributions). VAT (often on household goods) generates almost 17%. Onshore corporation tax (levied on the taxable profits of limited companies and other organisations) is forecast to deliver a further 7.2% in 2018–19 (OBR, 2018, *Tax by Tax, Spend by Spend*). In 2016, total tax receipts in the UK were 33.2% of GDP – less than the OECD average of 34.3% (OECD, 2017: 1). Returning to Figure 3.5, finance and housing delivered a tenth of these receipts, though this is only a small fraction of tax revenue attributable or related to property. Finance is a hugely profitable sector: tax receipts from this sector are equivalent to more than 35% of its GVA (compared to just over 21% for manufacturing) (OBR, 2011: 89). Although it is extremely difficult to discretely attribute tax income to land and property, given the complex relationship between economic activity and fixed assets (illustrated in this chapter's focus on capital switch and financialisation), these data point to the critical role that land and property plays in generating revenues and paying for public obligations. The UK generates twice as much tax revenue from 'property' as the

OECD average: rising property values (or the rising total asset value of the economy) deliver growth in that tax contribution, which is magnified by the significance of housing-related financial services and construction.

One important property-related tax that has not been examined in this section is local Council Tax. Gross council tax receipts across the UK in 2010–11 totalled almost £30 billion (OBR, 2012: 1) and were forecast to rise to nearly £35 billion by 2016–17. This tax generates significant revenues in support of *local services* but does not track rising property values: it seeks a contribution to local budgets and is linked only weakly to imputed rent. Levied rates are based on a valuation undertaken in 1991. Until it was abolished for homeowners in 1963, Schedule A tax was based on a 1936 valuation (Thatcher, 1960). Tax liability for homeowners does not track value uplift from purchase to sale, causing a number of problems in the housing market – as well as fairness issues between those who own housing, and benefit from imputed rent, and those who do not – that are picked up again later in this book. To be clear, the concern above has been with economic activities and services associated with property, including construction and debt-trading. This source of revenue is distinct from the *direct* capture of land rent, from which certain other countries derive public funds.

From homes to assets

Housing's economic context is certainly more complex than suggested in this chapter. Here, I have focused on the general importance of housing (and real estate more broadly) to UK economic output, directly and indirectly through the businesses for which it provides a core focus. These range from construction companies through to banks which lend, and therefore derive income and profit from, domestic mortgages. Sitting behind the banks are the financial service providers that trade in the securities backed by those mortgages. Housing, as Lord Beaverbrook explained, also sits centre stage in a broader production economy. Its consumption generates the need for an extensive range of associated goods and services. But in the last 50 years, the economic function of housing has transformed. While it remains a focus for construction activity, it has become increasingly important to a growing financial services sector. Housing production and consumption has been privatised: the rise of owner-occupation has accelerated the demand for residential mortgages, finance for which has been raised from the capital markets. This chapter has focused on particular aspects and outcomes of the transformation, including associated economic restructuring, investment flows (largely bank lending) and heightened reliance on tax revenues from property-related activities. The point is that housing is increasingly connected to broader economic 'wellbeing' and funds a full range of social goods. Tackling the 'housing crisis' will involve addressing the economic questions – and imbalances – arising from increased reliance on asset-based nominal growth.

The importance of investment in housing, directly through the buying and selling of homes and also indirectly through trading in mortgage-backed debt, means, in short, that housing is more asset than home. This is a broad claim, open to challenge: people's psychological attachment to place and to home remains strong. Many would dispute that housing's primary function is as asset. But seen from an economic perspective, it is clear that housing and the land it sits on has become a mainstay of economic growth. Even at an individual level, personal finances over time are healthier or weaker depending on one's housing status: owning a home, and benefiting from value appreciation, means being able to support children through their education and gives confidence in retirement. For many, housing is an asset to fall back on. This basic function has perhaps been neglected in this chapter – with its focus on the broader canvas and on flows of capital from the primary circuit of production to the secondary circuit of the built environment.

But it is those flows that contribute to the increasing cost of accessing housing, which has been opened up in new ways to asset-seeking capital. The positive feedback cycle, between house prices and loan credit (now supported by finance raised in capital markets) sees prices driven upwards and new supply unable to keep pace (with capital's demand for an expanded 'consumption fund'). On the 'plus side', loan credit and housing supply scarcity drives up asset prices, inflates taxable returns to investors and raises public revenues. But on the 'down side', workplace earnings cannot keep pace with rising prices – as those prices are calibrated to the levels of capital switching described above.

The economic crisis, of which the housing crisis is a part, is one in which nominal growth in total asset value is not supported by increased productivity in the real economy. One important marker of this crisis is the UK's slow wage growth. While some attribute this to austerity and public sector pay caps, Paul Johnson, Director of the Institute for Fiscal Studies, observes that low UK productivity in 2018 means that 'the amount we produce for each hour we work is basically the same as it was in 2008. If we're not producing any more, we're not in the end going to be able to earn any more' (BBC News, 2018c). The creation of wealth, dependent on control of land rents, has become detached from the productive capacity of the economy: wages stagnate while the pot of wealth stored in housing (and house prices) grows. Ryan-Collins et al (2017: 170), citing Armstrong (2016: F5), note that 'housing is by far the single largest source of wealth. In 2014 the value of households' and non-profit institutions' dwellings was £4.43 trillion – 58% of the entire net wealth of the UK'. The picture is similar in other countries: Western wealth is in assets and not in economic productivity. And as the wealth of property owners increases, the wages of workers stagnate, meaning that those reliant on workplace earnings are increasingly unlikely to become property owners themselves, and are therefore unable to share in the dubious benefits of this new form of economic growth and wealth creation.

However, housing's economic context is one in which there is still deep hostility towards any interventions or reforms that would move house prices from their upward track. Over several decades, sustained growth in homeownership has been a source of support for the status quo: "British people want our homes to go up in value" (Osborne, 2014). The constituency of voters wanting to see a change in direction has been traditionally small (Ryan-Collins et al, 2017), although this may change in the years ahead as inequality grows and the effects of the housing crisis continue to bite. But if commodification (and the transformation of housing into asset) is the source of stress, then some retreat from that commodification would seem to offer the only route from the current predicament. How this could be achieved without steps to direct capital back into productive activities – reversing the economic imbalance examined in this chapter – and away from land and property is perhaps difficult to imagine. Means can be identified, and are considered towards the end of this book, but implementation would involve overcoming deeply vested interest in pursuit of a redefined public good. If facilitating 'political strategies for de-commodification and re-communalisation of urban housing and infrastructure' (Wetzstein, 2017: 3169) proves to be too much of a stretch, then perhaps an achievable goal is to prevent, or slow the pace of, further commodification. This might be possible if residential land and development in England were refocused on the delivery of housing services as opposed to investment opportunities.

4

Local pathways to crisis

The last chapter explored the housing crisis's broader economic context. There are important structural reasons why capital has switched into property and housing: new capital pathways, which are now well established, are key drivers of national and local housing stress in many advanced economies. But it is also the case that, over a long period of time, different countries have taken different decisions in relation to the planning and regulation of housing and housing markets. They have also developed their own non-market responses to housing stress, viewing housing as more or less a 'private matter' and developing public responses to shifting patterns of housing need. The purpose of this chapter is to consider different explanations (or 'formulations') of the housing crisis: the local pathways which have led to this point. Those pathways are important because belief in their significance underpins opinion concerning the types of responses that are needed. If housing stress, for example, evidences market failure, then possible responses include a) deregulation aimed at achieving market efficiency, b) extended reregulation that seeks to 'correct' (endemic) failure, or c) a shift into non-market responses. Few people believe that the market is 'working well' in relation to housing. But preferred remedies have deep ideological roots: some believe that the market can be made to work well; others that it cannot. The most common analysis of the housing crisis is that new housing supply is inadequate relative to demand. Politicians of all stripes see a supply response as being important. But while those on the left see a role for an enlarged public sector in delivering extra homes, those on the right regularly argue that private enterprise should be freed from the dead hand of regulation: less planning will mean more housing. The broader nature of the 'supply debate' was flagged in Chapter 1 and is touched upon again later in this chapter. Likewise, more is said about planning in Chapter 6.

Local pathways/formulations

The objective now, however, is to consider the diversity of 'local pathways' to crisis in England. An overarching emphasis on building more homes is obviously key and features in many narratives, but it was the Royal Town Planning Institute (RTPI) that, in 2007, sought to broaden housing debate in England. It did so in reaction to mounting criticism of the planning system's role in restricting housing availability and driving up prices. Low housing affordability, it claimed, is a product of many factors that have nothing (or little) to do with planning control. Housing supply (the amount of existing and new housing) in a bounded space is necessarily finite and price movement will be set by activity in the second-hand market given that fewer than 15% of sale transactions each year are in the new-build sector. Within the second-hand sector, homeowners are borrowing against the value of their homes, extending and improving them – working to increase the value of their asset, in part because of 'perceived and actual deficiencies in personal pensions' (RTPI, 2007: 2). More money is being ploughed into the existing stock, creating a political context in which monetary (property) value must be defended and even essential new-build projects are locally rejected. That rejection, instrumentalised through planning, has a broad range of causes. Defence of asset value is important – as Coelho et al (2017) have recently demonstrated, by linking local authority rejection of new housing to concentrations of owner-occupation – but so too is the quality of schemes coming forward or lack of concern for their impacts on local services and amenity (Gurran et al, 2016).

The RTPI also drew attention to the price effects of buyer subsidies – key worker initiatives in the 2000s but also *Help to Buy* later on. A range of investment pressures were also said to have disruptive impacts on housing access in many areas: from second home purchases, through homes left empty, to *buy-to-let* investments (with mortgage advances in this sector rising from 44,000 in 1999 to 330,000 by 2006), and also increasing numbers of short lets, which reduced the availability of longer-term tenancies (this was before the advent of Airbnb rentals and their documented impacts on housing markets – see Gurran, 2018). Lending practices, including preference for advancing loans on property and land, were also viewed as important. Land values were seen as an underlying driver of the housing crisis, often being pushed up by speculative practices: trading in land with planning permission prior to its development, or 'banking' land and watching its value rise rather than developing it (this was the RTPI's main focus here, but with other factors flagged 'in no order of priority' (RTPI, 2007: 2) so as to obscure its full-frontal attack on the development sector). And finally, the overheating of some local markets was also, interestingly, attributed to the distribution of good and outstanding state schools and the generally uneven pattern of investment in pre-18 education. The point being made by the RTPI was that the housing crisis has a complex recipe of ingredients, and that analysis of the crisis should look beyond the obvious and delve more deeply into the interplay of factors. It was also looking to shift attention away from land use regulation and towards demand-side pressures and market processes.

A number of other authors have offered perspectives on the underlying causes of housing stresses – declining affordability reflected in reduced access to housing for a broad range of socioeconomic groups – and laid out what they view as dominant pathways along which the housing crisis has been reached. The purpose of this chapter is to examine the *principal formulations* of the housing crisis before considering if and how they fit together in any coherent way. For clarity, each formulation is presented as a proposition. Each proposition is then explained, with reference to relevant literature and data. The propositions are set out below and ahead of the main analysis, so as to provide a clear framework for the rest of the chapter:

Propositions behind the main formulations of the housing crisis

Proposition 1: Too few homes are being built in England and this is leading to rising prices and limited opportunities for people to find and access the housing they need. Responsibility for this lies in (private sector) construction capacity, the business models and practices of developers, and in planning regulation – underpinned by the way in which land for housing is allocated (see Chapter 1) and, in some instances, by popular local rejection of development.

Proposition 2: The pattern of housing demand has changed: overseas buyers and direct investors are eating into the supply of housing, causing a crisis centred on London (and other hotspots), which is rippling out to other parts of the country.

Proposition 3: As a country, we are too reliant on the private sector to supply the homes we need. Greater output and choice was achieved when the state was directly involved in building affordable homes, which were bureaucratically allocated and shielded from creeping privatisation in the form of the *right to buy*.

Proposition 4: Moreover, as a country we are too reliant on one type of private sector output: *build to sell*. New models from that sector (including '*build to rent*') and other social and collective approaches to housing provision (including community land trusts and greater opportunities to move away from speculative build to self-build, for example) could extend access to good housing and, in some instances, address issues arising from the private ownership of land and the private capture of land rent.

Proposition 5: The tax treatment of housing is hindering supply (for example, VAT – value-added tax – on conversion), impeding market function (for example, stamp duty adding upfront costs on purchase) and driving rising demand for housing over other assets (for example, removal of Schedule A tax in the past, application of capital gains tax and inheritance tax, and the structure of council tax), with implications for the wider economy.

Proposition 6: Increased credit supply and money creation (achieved through financial deregulation) has been part of an economic strategy designed to activate new housing demand and consumption in support of the 'productive economy' and also the service-based economy (particularly financial services). This has had the effect of pumping new money/capital into the available housing supply and pushing prices out of the reach of households on average incomes – and even higher earners in some areas.

Proposition 7: Returning to Proposition 1, above, housebuilding (and transaction activity – see Beauregard, 1994) responds to money (credit) supply and not simply to housing need. The housing crisis is a disequilibrium between the supply of money and the supply of the housing asset. For those in need, this leads to declining affordability and a crisis of access. But at the centre of this is the intentional refunction of the relationship between housing and the economy. This draws in overseas buyers (Proposition 2), privileges the private sector (Proposition 3) and owner-occupation (Proposition 4), functions on the basis of privileged tax treatment (Proposition 5), and is underpinned by the supply of credit/debt (Proposition 6).

One apparent flaw in Proposition 7 – which attempts to integrate different formulations – is that the supply of credit seems not to have driven up housing supply. But access to credit is not evenly distributed; rather, it is restricted to those with collateral against which to borrow. Existing homeowners can remortgage, release equity, and invest in home improvements and extensions that increase the value of their property. They can also secure mortgages for *buy-to-let* or second homes. While the proportion of all households who are owner-occupiers has declined in England, the proportion of homeowners with more than one property has increased (Resolution Foundation, 2017). Credit is also advanced to those with property portfolios against which to borrow. Existing home owners can lever more credit than those without collateral, and they pursue housing as the asset investment of choice (and are encouraged to do so) for the other reasons set out in Proposition 7. Credit drives supply by pushing up house prices and hence the incentive to develop land, to the extent that expected profit margins are maintained. Moreover, unequal access to credit has expanded demand for housing, as *asset*, among those who already enjoy the benefits of housing as *home*. Financialisation, as described by Harvey (1978), Beauregard (1994), Gotham (2006, 2009) and others, is often manifest in increased transaction activity in the existing built environment (of commercial property and homes), and in the bidding-up of prices, rather than in the production of new property. The propositions are now more fully explored.

Proposition 1

Too few homes are being built in England and this is leading to rising prices and limited opportunities for people to find and access the housing they need. Responsibility for this lies in (private sector) construction capacity, the business models and practices of developers, and in planning regulation – underpinned by the way in which land for housing is allocated and, in some instances, by popular local rejection of development.

The housing supply debate – or the general view that the housing crisis will be *mostly* remedied by building more homes – sees housing demand as knowable and linked largely to utility (households forming, having children, and demanding housing in proximity to schools and other services). Failure to supply homes for forming households is a more tangible housing crisis than one linked to finance, credit, pensions or other abstractions.

Acceptance that more homes need to be built – because national completions are lower than projections of household formation (see Figure 4.1) – is followed by a questioning of why they are not being built. What is happening on the production side (what are developers doing?) and what responsibility does land-use planning have for current levels of output? Acceptance that patterns of economic

Figure 4.1: Housebuilding and net housing supply, 2006/07 to 2015/16, compared with household formation projections, 2014–39

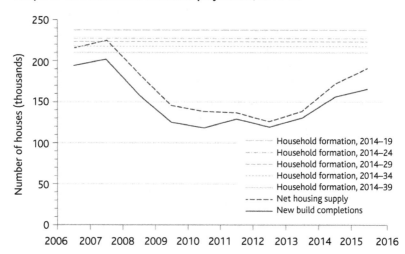

Note: Household formation lines refer to average annual rate for shorter to longer periods.
Source: Bentley, 2016: 3; citing DCLG Table 120 and 'Household Projections, England, 2014–39'

opportunity determine where people need to live leads to another follow-on question: how do local and regional patterns of supply relate to demand – where people need and want to live (see Figure 4.2)?

The supply debate therefore has two main components, which implicate producers and regulators in the problem of inadequate housing production. The producers (largely volume housebuilders, responsible for 80% of total output) either won't or can't supply the homes that are needed. If they *won't* then this is likely to be due to dominant business interest (making money) conflicting with the aspiration of others (government, which sees the private sector as its principal instrument of housing delivery): essentially, there is some reason why it is better to build fewer than more homes. If they *can't*, then this is likely to be due to labour capacity, availability of materials, access to finance or regulatory constraint. Regulatory constraint – the role, principles and practices of land-use planning – may generate uncertainty, risk and make it more difficult to raise finance on more marginal development sites (de Magalhaes et al, 2018). Alternatively, some of the land being allocated for new housing in local plans is unsuited to that use in the current market: there is too much political influence over those allocations, which are intentionally unrealistic and designed to slow the pace of development. Government inspectors will pick this up at local inquiries but still, political manoeuvring –

Figure 4.2: Net housing supply, 2015/16, as a percentage of projected annual household formation, 2014–39, by local authority

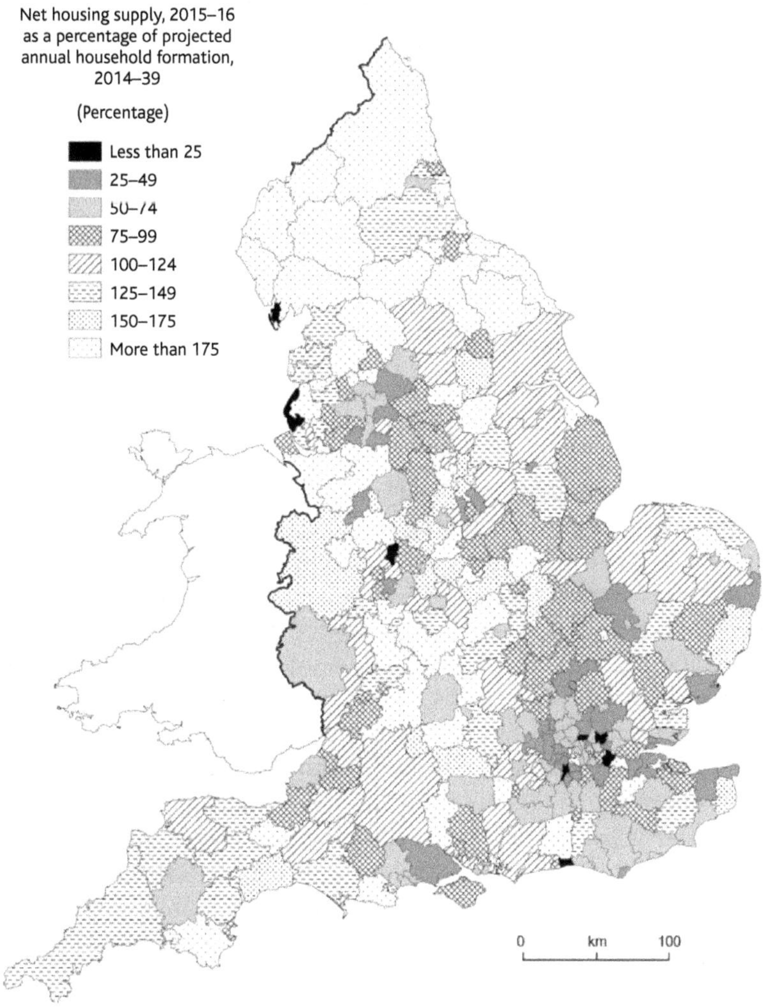

Net housing supply, 2015–16
as a percentage of projected
annual household formation,
2014–39

(Percentage)

■ Less than 25
▨ 25–49
▨ 50–74
▨ 75–99
▨ 100–124
▨ 125–149
▨ 150–175
▢ More than 175

0   km   100

Source: Bentley, 2016: 5; citing DCLG Tables 122 and 425 and Civitas calculations

politicians representing antidevelopment constituencies – will add a new dimension to regulatory 'drag'.

Figure 4.3 presents the number of planning permissions granted in England in each of the last ten years against the number of new homes built. It shows that permissions are higher than completions. How should this be interpreted? A recent study by Lichfields (2017) has explored this issue and addresses the question of 'land banking': developers 'choosing not to promote or build out sites, and instead

Figure 4.3: Completions and permissions

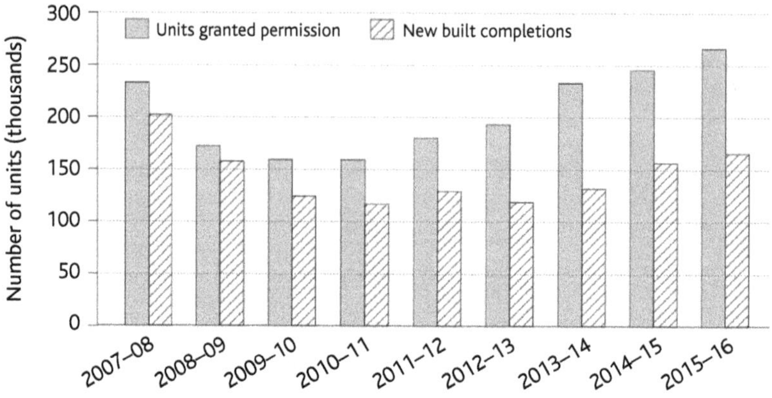

Source: Halligan, 2018

sitting back and watching the value of the land grow, before eventually building new homes, or selling the site on at an inflated price to another party' (Lichfields, 2017: 3). The authors note that other studies have refuted the accusation of land banking (p. 8) and their own conclusion is that lapse rates, between permissions obtained and completions achieved, happen for a number of reasons – and lag, between the same events, has numerous explanations. Lapses occur because of difficulties raising finance, because it may not ultimately be worth developing a site, because of the time taken to meet pre-commencement conditions or because a developer's priorities change. Practical start may be delayed by changing market conditions or other contextual factors. This means that it is unrealistic to 'expect that 100% of homes will be delivered from 100% of planning permissions granted in any given location' (Lichfields, 2017: 12). But likewise, 'given the significant costs and risks involved in land promotion, construction and sales ... there is unlikely to be a business case for active land banking that "games" the system in order to suppress housing supply' (p. 1). Turning the term on its head, Lichfields conclude that land banking is essential for achieving additional housing supply, because across the stock of permissions, just 50% will be converted to completions in a given year. With various assumptions about lapse and lag rates, the study points to a need for many more planning permissions in support of government's current target to deliver a net addition of 300,000 homes per year.

While the planning system needs to increase the stock of permissions, neither that system nor the behaviour of housebuilders seems to be an unsurmountable impediment to supply. Lapse and lag rates are due to various practicalities of site buildout and market conditions. Supply is important and the delivery of new housing can be expected to address *shortages* where they arise, for example, in areas experiencing employment growth or where the past rate of development has not kept pace with population rises and migration. Places often need new housing; and vacancies and churn in the existing stock will not meet all needs, even where levels of 'inessential' consumption are low. Bentley (2016: 4) points to a failure in many English local authority areas, especially in the southeast of England, to match housebuilding rates to projected household formation (see Figure 4.2). New supply is *part of* the housing cost puzzle, which is examined more closely at the end of this section.

In his analysis of the 'housing supply crisis' in England, Bowie (2017: 26) looks briefly at different perspectives on observable housing tensions. He categories these as a) a neoliberal thesis, which generally views 'the bureaucratic and constraining planning system' as a central cause of inadequate housing delivery; b) a distributional argument, which claims adequacy in housing supply – but unequal distribution; and c) the 'financialisation of capital' thesis which, for various reasons sees economic shift as key to the housing crisis. Bowie's view is that 'no single theory provides a satisfactory contextualisation' (2017: 26), but it is clear that the neoliberal explanation targets the issue of supply, seeing land-use planning – and the exclusion of land from development, including in areas of green belt – as central to the housing crisis. For that reason, the emphasis on new supply perhaps requires further comment, building on the introduction provided earlier.

At the heart of the *supply thesis* (that is, the view that new, open-market, supply is inadequate and increasing that supply will solve the housing crisis) is, again, the assumption that demand is knowable/calculable, spatially bounded and underpinned by a need for housing services (utility). Thereafter, the solution to the declining affordability, falling rates of homeownership, homelessness and general inequality flagged in the opening chapter must lie in the building of more homes. And increased supply relative to measured demand is achievable, by and large, through reduced land use regulation. Projections of household formation are generally thought to accurately reveal the level of future housing demand across the UK. Formation rates are regularly presented alongside other data (for example, housing starts and completions – again, see Figure 4.1 above) to reveal demand/supply mismatches that are then used to explain rising house prices and inadequate access. For example, the Lyons Review of Housing Supply has claimed that 'we need to build at least 243,000 homes a year to keep up with the number of new households being formed, but last year we only built 109,000 homes [and] without a change of course, it is predicted that the country will be short of up to two million homes by 2020' (Lyons, 2014: 6). The opening figure has unacknowledged limitations: it is a guess at the extent of newly arising demand for 'housing services' that will be activated by forming households with the capacity to pay market prices and rents. It fails to capture broader demands on the housing stock – from domestic and overseas investors, purchasers of second homes and so on – inferring instead that demand is bounded (in space) and activated only by the need to be housed. The broader nature of demand was introduced in the opening chapter and suggests that this inference is flawed.

An appreciation of the origins of household projections helps explain their continuing value and their increasing limitations. After the Second World War, a methodology was developed for translating population figures – previously used to keep track of future public pension eligibility – into household projections (Gallent, 2005). These became a key planning tool at a time when local authorities and New Town Development Corporations were advancing significant public housing programmes: they provided a measure of the future requirement for a largely non-marketised product being delivered as part of more comprehensive state welfare (Gallent, 2016). The subsequent privatisation of housing production and consumption – alongside the refunctioning of housing as asset and emergent and unbounded patterns of demand – has strained the connection between projections and requirement. Because they track the mix of households forming and the age profile of the population, projections provide an important tool for estimating future healthcare needs, school place demand and pension costs. But these, in large part, remain public goods. The challenge in relation to housing is that need does not link neatly to household formation. A proportion of demand is expressed by non-residents: domestic second home buyers in some locations, international investors in others. Projections provide a 'starting point' for estimating housing requirements but only if 'market evidence is given proper weight' (Whitehead, 2016: 417).

They have also provided key intelligence for public housing programmes, but are less useful today for predicting patterns of market demand and consumption. However, they remain important in public and political discourse. The headline projection figure (noted in Lyons, 2014) is taken to be the amount of housing that the country should be building. But while it underscores the need to deliver new housing in some areas, it does not reveal the scale of building required to progress an effective supply response in the absence of any demand-side interventions (in levels of mortgage lending or tax adjustments). In order to meet demand without seeking to manage that demand or divert investment pressure to other assets, building rates will need to significantly exceed household formation for a sustained and extended period (HBF, 2014), requiring 'output levels of well over 400,000 per annum over many years', according to Whitehead (2016: 419).

That capital movements (into housing) and imbalances in market power (leading to more housing being concentrated in fewer hands) are implicated in the crisis has been a difficult pill for successive right-leaning, centre-right and even centre-left governments to swallow. Housing's current role in capitalist production, described in the last chapter, cannot be easily shifted. This has made government highly receptive to anti-regulation sentiment and calls to speed up the planning process (see Barker, 2006). Broadly, it has been easier to incentivise housebuilding while presenting the crisis as the product of a market held back by overzealous bureaucracy: ordinary 'working families' pitted against outdated and synthetic regulation. This formulation of the housing crisis, conforming to Bowie's neoliberal thesis, provides governments with achievable goals during a single parliamentary term: release public land for private development and undertake showcase reforms of the planning system. The period of peak housing crisis in England has been accompanied by frenzied planning reforms which, since 2010, have been billed as simplifications aimed at facilitating housing growth (Clarke, 2012). They have been built on critiques of the planning system that have laid blame for rising prices at its door (Nathan and Overman, 2011).

Those critiques have a long history, beginning with Hall and Colleagues' seminal *The Containment of Urban England* (1973), which warned that postwar planning and urban containment – in the form of green belt – had been a victory for the rural shires, with their green fields and their NIMBYs, and a defeat for overcrowded towns and cities. Much later, Peter Hall launched another stinging attack on urban containment in defence of 'rural land': 'There is a good reason and a bad reason for more compact urban development. The bad one is to save rural land. It is bad because there is no reason to do so, either now or in the foreseeable future' (Hall, 2001: 101). He went on to describe how, in the mid-1990s, 10% of land in the southeast of England had been in EU set-aside, 'growing nothing but weeds' (p. 101). Similar critiques were aired in Alan Evans' 1991 analysis of housing standards and affordability: restrictive planning was supported by several 'myths' about England's development capacity and the priority given to environmental protection. Inevitably, planning constraint can impede housing supply and, in doing so, raise access barriers. Given that planning decisions are rooted in local politics – generating what Barker (2004) termed an 'implementation gap' in housing delivery – as well as land use and national priorities, it seems inevitable that the rate of housebuilding can be impacted upon, locally and in aggregate. Indeed, suggestions that the housing crisis is mainly about planning (see, for example, Cheshire, 2009; Hilber and Vermeulen, 2010; Hilber, 2015) have found a ready audience in policy circles, largely because they align with recent governments' preference for deregulation. Such deregulation and reregulation, however, is a double-edged sword, sustaining a level of *global* demand for housing through its support for financialisation (via bank reregulation and by engineering a secondary mortgage market that has increased the flow of credit into housing) that cannot be met through *local* supply even in the context of much looser planning. Cheshire et al (2014) agree with the point made above: that household projections offer a partial view of housing requirement. But while they see rising house prices (and increasing housing space consumption) as being determined by increases in workplace earnings (more housing needs to be built to keep pace with the aspirations made attainable by those earnings), other processes – including capital movements – would seem to be having a more significant effect on a *privatised* housing system today than they were when either Hall and colleagues or Evans were commenting on the importance of planning and the size of the available housing stock 30 to 50 years ago. Likewise, housing supply/planning regulation are but one of a number of determinants of house prices.

Before moving on to consider other formulations of the housing crisis, a brief detour into price setting – which is pertinent to all formulations – would perhaps be useful. House prices are, largely, driven by the trading of property within the *existing housing stock* because the volume of transactions in that segment of the market is greater than in the new-build segment. Some of that trading is speculative: 'the buying and selling of properties in order to exploit ... escalating markets feed a rise in property values that encourages further speculative activity' (Beauregard, 1994: 730). It is also backed by mortgage credit: different buyers using money from the banks to bid against one another and bid up prices. New build – even when new supply targets are achieved – represents on average no more than 1% of that built stock (Bramley and Watkins, 2016: 8), meaning that the relationship between additional housebuilding and price change, observed at a neighbourhood level, can be minimal and short-term (Whitehead et al, 2015: 4). That said, modelling has suggested statistically significant price effects in some situations (Bramley and Leishman, 2005). Muellbauer and Murphy (2008: 10), for example, have built models that predict falls of between 1.5% and 2% across regions where a 1% net increase in housing stock is achieved, relative to working-age population. Obviously, building homes where it is not needed will not impact on prices – hence the point that building rates need to track, and spatially relate to, changes in the number of workers and working households. But overall, and assuming that building does take place in the right locations, the 1% net increase is roughly the 300,000 homes nationally that commentators generally agree need to be built (achievable if there is a constant stock of around 600,000 live permissions). Achieving that target will start to flatten the market. Doing more than flattening the market – that is, substantially changing the ratio between earnings and house prices, and hence tackling affordability – through *housebuilding alone* will require a much higher build rate and a commensurately enlarged stock of permissions. This is because we would be trying to overpower and counteract other determinants of house prices (and affordability) through a new supply response.

Such apparent 'oversupply' relative to measures of demand rooted in demography (which miss broader demands on the housing stock in some areas) seems to offer a way of restoring a degree of market equilibrium. But trying to satiate the market's appetite for housing by turning on the supply tap, and leaving it running, poses significant risks. In the years leading up to the 2008 GFC, England's more cautious (aka slow and cumbersome) land-use planning system meant that unlike some of its European neighbours – notably the Republic of Ireland and Spain – the UK did not experience a boom in housebuilding, triggered by relaxed lending, low interest rates and soaring demand for real estate. In those countries, frenzied building activity – often in odd locations – resulted in bankruptcies and loan defaults that deepened the crisis for Irish and Spanish banks (Duca et al, 2010; Dolphin and Griffith, 2011). That activity was responding not to population growth or changes in household structure (that is, an underlying *trend*) – supported by earnings growth and, in turn, to rising productivity – but rather to the surge in investment (as capital shifted into real estate) that ebbs and flows in a potentially volatile way, even if there appears to be greater permanence in that flow than there was half a century ago.

The point here is that real house prices, which rise and fall at different times, are determined not only by the size of the housing stock relative to working-age population, but by a range of other trend-based and cyclical drivers. Meen (2011: 357) contrasts more predictable factors affecting real house prices (including those viewed as stable and knowable, such as the tax treatment of housing and planning regulation) with those which are more volatile and linked to economic cycles and, increasingly, the global interconnectedness of economies. Hence, income (including workplace earnings), interest rates, credit availability (and lender assessments of risk), wealth accumulation and movement (across borders), expected capital gains from one asset compared to another, changing labour and construction costs, and rates of economic activity all impact on prices, on the cost of housing relative to earnings and on affordability. Crucially, opportunities exist to influence all of these cyclical factors through economic policy, potentially changing their relationship with housing and house prices.

Proposition 2

The pattern of housing demand has changed: overseas buyers and investors are eating into the supply of housing, causing a crisis centred on London (and other hotspots), which is rippling out to other parts of the country.

The direct acquisition of housing as pure asset has been an important narrative in recent housing debate. The general story here is that overseas buyers, with 'cash to splash', have been attracted to the London housing market. They have seen and grasped an opportunity to achieve significant capital and revenue returns, through buying, selling and renting out property in the capital – especially in 'prime' locations where housing is highly sought-after. Some of those buyers vent their demand for housing in London because investment opportunities at home are more constrained or because political situations are judged to be less stable: risks are greater and returns more uncertain. The Hong Kong housing market, for example, is highly constrained (Gurran et al, 2016). Building land is scarce (and often needs to be reclaimed from the sea at substantial cost) and homebuyers/investors are reluctant to cross the border into neighbouring Shenzhen. London, with its historic links to Hong Kong, appears to offer an ideal investment outlet: housing is high quality, relatively cheap and offers good returns. The circumstances faced by investors in Singapore are very similar: land is constrained and few are interested in crossing the causeway into Malaysia. Much better returns are achievable in London, to which there are similar historic links and, nowadays, excellent flight connections. In other parts of the world – notably Russia and the Middle East – vast sums of money are now concentrated in relatively few hands. Ultra-high-net-worth individuals in those countries often look to London as a stable and secure place to park their wealth, confident in the knowledge that successive UK governments and London mayors have welcomed their direct investments in real estate, keen to have these 'supports' for the London property market as well as the wider spending (and VAT receipts) that this global elite bring to the city.

This narrative then extends to cover the wider market impacts of this direct investment: prices escalating in London prime property before rippling out to other attractive locations and then into the wider southeast of England and beyond – as house-price refugees flee the capital's overheating market, taking their own money to new places (and sometimes gentrifying those places, triggering new stages of residential displacement).

London is a world city and there seems little doubt that global interest in its residential property market is impacting on house prices and housing affordability. But how big is that impact? There have been several studies of overseas investment buying during the last few years. Some of these have been concerned with broader market impacts; others have focused on the role of 'inward investment' in supporting the new-build sector. Rossall Valentine (2015: 46) looks at what he calls the 'foreign ownership problem', which extends not only to housing but the sale of 'iconic British brands' to overseas buyers during the last 30 years or so. Foreign ownership of housing is viewed as part of a broader pattern of investment demand that is locking ordinary families out of the housing market. Although some care is taken to present foreign ownership as just a segment of that demand, there is a clear sense that *British* housing and the *British* people are suffering at the hands of wealthy *foreigners*:

> The UK housing market is at present grossly unbalanced between powerful investors and weak owner-occupiers. The future for British people who are not already on the housing market is grim and getting worse as British housing increasingly becomes the preferred global haven for wealthy foreigners to invest their money ... the UK market is now rigged against owner-occuppership, with the result that many British people not currently on the housing ladder are condemned to never being able to buy a house in their own country. (Rossall Valentine, 2015: 55)

A distinction is made between the impacts arising from the purchase of second-hand property and new build, with Rossall Valentine arguing that a 'new only' rule should be introduced (2015: 53), limiting foreign purchase to new homes. Other authors have been far more circumspect about the impact of overseas direct investors on the UK and London housing markets. While Rossall Valentine chooses to single out wealthy foreigners, others have argued that these are bit players in wider patterns of housing demand. Scanlon et al (2017a: 8) note that 'much of the analysis of overseas purchases of London property focuses on prime and super-prime units, although these account for very small numbers'. Quoting figures from *London First*, they point out that in 2012 just 750 of 97,000 new build sales (1%) went to international second home buyers. Moreover, just 8% of all transactions in London are focused on prime property and only a small fraction of these involved overseas buyers. In other words, the interactions of 'wealthy foreigners' with both the new-build and second-hand sectors is relatively small. Figures are presented below.

The problem, perhaps, with overseas buyers – and the reason for interest in them – is that they are implicated in London's housing crisis at a time when that crisis is particularly acute. By juxtaposing stories of young people struggling with rising housing costs with accounts of profiteering from those same rising costs, media reporting contributes to the sense that housing has become central to a wider pattern of social injustice. Besides the broader issue of foreign ownership, the BBC reported in January 2018 that 97,000 UK properties are owned by offshore companies – 23,000 of those by entities registered in the British Virgin Islands (Verity, 2018). Of the total, 44% are in London: 11,500 in the City of Westminster and 6,000 in Kensington and Chelsea. Not all of the owners of those 'entities' will be foreign. Some will be UK citizens who, up until April 2017, could avoid inheritance tax by owning property through an offshore entity registered in a (usually British) tax haven. Usefully, in its report on this issue, the BBC provided a mapping tool for drilling down and identifying individual properties owned by offshore firms: using that tool, I discovered that my own rented house is owned by a company registered in Cyprus.

Because ownership through an offshore company may conceal the nationality of an owner, and because tax status – domiciled or non-domiciled – is arguably more important than whether an owner is 'foreign by birth', the data on overseas housing investment does not present an entirely clear picture of the role of 'wealthy foreigners' in the housing market. Most studies agree, however, that the role of such buyers has enlarged in recent years – the general narrative of increased interest in London property rings true.

Sassen (2014: 134) has observed that London appears more indiscriminately attractive to foreign investment than other locations, with capital flowing into the city from across the globe. And while studies continue to underscore the draw of prime and super-prime locations (see Civitas, 2014; Atkinson et al, 2016a, 2016b, 2017), the overseas market now extends into some parts of outer London. This point is made by Wallace et al (2017). Like the Scanlon et al (2017a) study – which responded to a brief from the Greater London Authority – their interest is in the new-build market (and who occupies *new homes* in London). Between April 2014 and March 2016, 13% of new build sales were to overseas buyers (Wallace et al, 2017: 7). Almost 50% of those sales were to buyers from Hong Kong and Singapore (2017: 8). The distribution of overseas sales, as a percentage of all new build sales, across the London boroughs is shown in Figure 4.4. The attraction of riverside property is revealed in the data, as is the

Figure 4.4: Proportion of all sales in each London Borough to overseas buyers

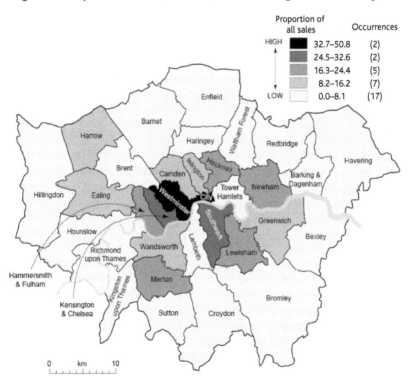

Source: Wallace et al, 2017: 10; citing Land Registry data

concentration of purchases in Westminster and in Kensington and Chelsea – the same boroughs with the highest concentrations of properties acquired through offshore companies. When the Mayor of London, Sadiq Khan, responded to growing concern over foreign buying in 2016, by commissioning research into the issue, he was careful to underscore the benefits of external investment in new housebuilding. Hence, the study by Scanlon et al (2017a) was steered to look broadly at four questions: what proportion of new residential units in London are sold to overseas buyers? What proportion of these are left empty (as so-called 'buy to leave' investments)? How reliant are London residential developers on off-plan sales to overseas buyers? And what role do major overseas investors (for example, pension funds) play in the residential development process?

Like Wallace et al (2017), the London School of Economics' (LSE) study (Scanlon et al, 2017a) reported a relatively low proportion of sales to overseas buyers. In fact, because of uncertainties in figures gained from estate agents, they deferred to Wallace and colleagues' 13% figure. Furthermore, they concluded that less than 1% of properties were left permanently empty – though 'for those units bought as second homes, occupancy could be as little as a few weeks a year' (2017a: 3). The big finding from the study – and the one that the mayor seemed to be angling for when he announced the GLA's intention to commission this research – was that:

> overseas buyers almost certainly contributed to the net availability of housing to Londoners. The positive impact of overseas investment on the supply of new housing development is additional and complementary to that arising from these sales and is becoming increasingly important in speeding delivery, especially on large sites. One important implication of these findings is that there would be real costs to the London housing market if overseas investment either through purchasing new dwellings or supporting new developments began to feel unwelcome. (Scanlon et al, 2017a: 29)

House price impacts arising from foreign purchasing of new homes were said to be slight given the price-setting role of new build relative to the sum of transactions across the market. Clearly, the study had limitations: it was confined to the new-build sector and it was steered to confirm the undoubted role of global development finance in supporting big, high-value and high-cost projects. Its findings are not surprising and will probably not assuage the fears of those who believe that foreign capital is complicit in the London housing crisis. However, setting aside the wider finance issues tackled by the study, it is clear that the aspiration to park wealth in housing is not confined to foreign elites, who are simply exploiting the opportunities afforded by the UK's open and loosely regulated property market – see Rossall Valentine (2015: 52) for an overview of regulatory actions taken by other countries. Domestic policy has long nurtured this aspiration and the movement of overseas wealth into housing may now be considered one further source of reassurance for UK homebuyers whose borrowing plans are shaped by expectations of rising prices.

Proposition 3

As a country, we are too reliant on the private sector to supply the homes we need. Greater output and choice was achieved when the state was directly involved in building affordable homes, which were bureaucratically allocated and shielded from creeping privatisation in the form of the right to buy.

The privatisation of the broader 'housing system' was produced, in part, by a rejection of the state's role in housing delivery in the last decades of the twentieth century. The narrative of declining public housing provision in the UK is a familiar one; the story has been recounted numerous times (see, for example, Cole and Furbey, 1994; Jones and Murie, 2006; Murie, 2016). The stock of public housing in the UK was built up over several decades with the decision to engage in 'state landlordism' taken at the end of the nineteenth century. However, the UK – alongside other European countries recovering from the devastation of the Second World War – accelerated its programme of public housebuilding after the war. The delivery of 'council housing' formed part of a new postwar social contract and a broader state welfare package that included the creation of the National Health Service in 1948 and a comprehensive planning system in the previous year. But from the 1950s onwards, local authorities were given the facility to sell council homes (following the Housing Act 1952; see Murie, 2016: 14). That facility became a *right to buy* for sitting tenants in 1980.

Local authorities and New Town Development Corporations built just over 4.9 million homes across the UK between 1949 and 1980 – just under half of all new homes built during that period (10 million

– MHCLG, Live Table 241[1]). Public housebuilding tailed off after 1980, with a further 373,000 built between 1981 and 2016 (5.5% of all homes built). During that same period, private enterprise delivered 5.5 million homes – nearly 82% of total output. Housing association output was 4.4% of the 1949–80 total, rising to nearly 13% for the 1981–2016 period. At its peak, in 1953, public housing output stood at 245,160 units – 75% of all units built during that year were 'council houses'. At its low point, in 2004, local authorities across the UK built just 130 new homes: 0.06% of total output. Figures for England can be provided separately (MHCLG, Live Table 244) but these merely reproduce the same peaks and troughs and the overall pattern of postwar growth and rapid decline after the Housing Act 1980 and the introduction of the *right to buy*, followed by stock transfers to the housing association sector.

Figure 4.5 shows the changing balance between public, housing association and private sector housebuilding between 1949 and 2016. But how much housing was 'lost' to the public sector following the introduction of the *right to buy*? In April 1981, the total stock of dwellings in England stood at 17.9 million. Of those, just over 5.1 million were rented from local authorities (29%). In March 2016, there were 23.7 million dwellings, of which 1.6 million were rented from local authorities (just under 7%). The net 'loss' of council homes

Figure 4.5: Housebuilding: permanent dwellings completed, by tenure

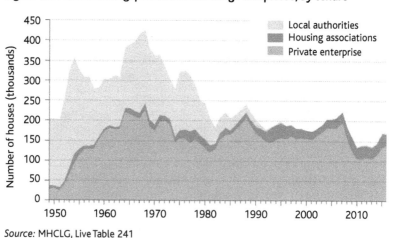

Source: MHCLG, Live Table 241

---

[1] MHCLG maintains live tables on key housing statistics. The root for these tables is: https://www.gov.uk/government/statistical-data-sets.

over that period – mainly because of transfer to other tenures – was just over 3.5 million units (MHCLG, Live Table 104). That figure rises to 4.1 million, in aggregate, for England, Scotland and Wales (MHCLG, Live Table 102). England, and the rest of the UK, has shifted from being a society content to build and live in council homes to one dominated by owner-occupation, private renting (62% and 20%, respectively, for Great Britain in 2016), and delivery by private enterprise (81% of housing completions across the UK in the same year). For stock and new build, we are roughly 80% private, with the remaining 20% dominated by third-sector providers.

What have been the consequences of this shift to private provision? The *right to buy* has accelerated the growth in UK home ownership. Murie (2016: 5) points out that two million former tenants purchased their homes under the *right to buy* (other tenancies transferred to housing associations) and because of available discounts, this 'initially expanded home ownership, but failed to sustain that growth, and some 40% of *right to buy* properties were transferred to private renting'. As noted in Chapter 3, the purchase of freeholds and leaseholds through the *right to buy* contributed to increased demand for mortgage lending, diverting 'investment from other areas and sectors' – thereby accentuating the economic shift away from manufacturing. The stock of 'bureaucratically allocated' housing across the UK has substantially declined: this housing was let on 'fair rents' and was affordable to households on a range of different incomes. It was allocated according to assessed need, using different points-based systems. And finally, its loss has resulted in a sharp turn away from bureaucratic allocation of housing in the UK to allocation mainly through 'the market'. This turn, according to Tunstall (2015), has been a significant cause of increasing housing inequality (see Figure 4.6). Over a hundred-year period (from 1911) she shows that the bureaucratic allocation of housing by the state during the twentieth century was associated with rising equality of housing/space access. The emphasis on market allocation since 1980, when the *right to buy* was introduced, has resulted in a reversal of those gains.

The consumption of a commodified housing resource through the market – and the shift away from bureaucratic allocation of council housing by local authorities – has led to a skewed distribution of the available housing 'space' in England (Tunstall, 2015). Building on general conclusions reached by Dorling (2014a), Tunstall adds weight to the argument that 'what appears to be a housing supply problem in the UK is really a housing distribution problem, driven by high and growing inequality in housing consumption' (Tunstall, 2015: 109).

Figure 4.6: Inequality in distribution of rooms per person in private households in England and Wales, Gini coefficient and proportion below 60% median space per person, 1911–2011

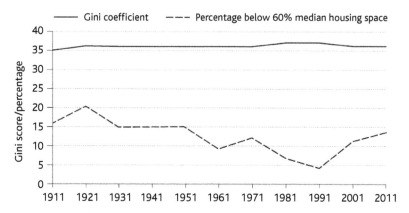

Source: Tunstall, 2015

That distribution problem is underpinned by income (and wealth) inequality and also by the association of 'big houses' with wealth and status. Between 1911 and 2011, 85.9 million extra rooms were created through development in England and Wales. The rate of development was faster than population increase and household formation. In 1911, 34.6 million residents shared 37.4 million rooms; a hundred years later, 54.8 million residents shared 123.3 million rooms (Tunstall, 2015: 114). The ratio of rooms to residents more than doubled. But while in 1911 just 2,639 residents were living on their own in ten or more rooms, in 2011 331,337 single people were living in eight or more rooms. The percentage of households living in less than 60% of the median housing space fell from just over 15% in 1911 to just under 5% in 1991, but then shot back up to just under 15% in 2011 (Tunstall, 2015: 117). Tunstall's analysis reveals that there is now more housing space in England and Wales per capita than there was a century ago, but the consumption of that space is skewed towards wealthy households largely because of the turn from bureaucratic to market allocation of housing. The improvements in space 'allocation' until 1981 can be explained by the prevalence of council housing, built and allocated bureaucratically. But increased reliance on market allocation after that date – as local authorities stopped building and started selling their stock of homes – meant that income inequality (also rising during this period – Dorling, 2014a) came to be mirrored in patterns of housing access and consumption.

Another important part of this narrative is the public sector's switch from building homes – *subsidising* 'bricks and mortar' – to subsidising individuals through a system of 'housing benefit'. That system, providing income support to households unable to otherwise meet social rents (in the third sector) or private rents, was viewed in the 1980s as a short- to medium-term cost of withdrawing from direct public provision – payable to workless or low-income recipients. However, because housing associations were unable (and never meant) to bridge the gap in social housing provision left by the loss of council housing, 'governments have been faced with increasing housing benefit costs associated with tenants paying market rents in the private sector because there was too little public and social rented housing available' (Murie, 2016: 5). Successive governments have become victims of their own housing crisis: privatisation and the various drivers of increasing housing costs – set out in this chapter and Chapter 3 – have locked government into the private rental market, with benefit payments spiralling upwards along with private rents. The BBC reported in 2016 that, in the previous five years, British local authorities had spent £3.5 billion on temporary accommodation for homeless households (BBC News, 2016). Because private enterprise has been focused on building homes for sale, the expansion of the private rental sector (rising from 11% of homes in England in 1981 to 20% in 2017) has largely occurred through 'amateur landlordism' – private individuals taking out *buy-to-let* mortgages (Pawson et al, 2017). Rising rents in the private sector, especially in the south of England, mean that growing numbers of working households now rely on housing benefit (Holmans, 2014). Dorling (2014b) has argued that by subsidising individuals rather than building homes, government has propagated a negative circularity, with former social housing tenants now reliant on a largely unregulated and often unaffordable private rental sector, sometimes paying their housing benefit to *buy-to-let* investors. This narrative, therefore, sees the money that was once spent on building homes redirected to private housing investment, widening the divide between homeowners and non-homeowners.

More broadly, the pattern of privatisation described in this section – alongside the loss of bureaucratically allocated housing – has increased households' exposure to market forces. Forms of affordable housing are still provided, but these are concerned with supporting *market entry*. They include housing let on 'affordable rents' that rise with income and provide limited shielding from full market costs. They also include intermediate tenures such as shared ownership, designed to allow assisted households on average incomes (or even well-above-average incomes in London) to 'staircase' into full ownership. Declining housing affordability and evidence of increased inequality in housing access has catalysed support for greater involvement of the public sector in housebuilding. On the left, there are calls to change direction and build council homes again. On the right, there is some support for greater involvement of local authorities in general housebuilding, as a means of increasing construction capacity and returning to the output peaks of the 1950s and 1960s, only achieved through a combination of public and private activity.

Proposition 4

As a country we are too reliant on one type of private sector output: build to sell. New models from that sector (including 'build to rent') and other social and collective approaches to housing provision (including community land trusts and greater opportunities to move away from speculative build to self-build, for example) could extend access to good housing and, in some instances, address issues arising from the private ownership of land and the private capture of land rent.

It was noted in the last section that more than 80% of new housing in the UK is delivered by private enterprise. Of the 171,000 homes built in 2016, the private sector was responsible for nearly 139,000. Ten housebuilders built more than half (76,587) of those homes and the top 25 largest housebuilders, by turnover, built 101,506 homes – 73% of total private output (Housebuilder, 2017). These companies are mainly engaged in '*build to sell*', either to owner-occupiers or *buy-to-let* investors. In the ten years to 2016, total output from private enterprise *in England* was 1,036,150 completions. During the same period, the number of owner-occupiers fell by 31,000 (MHCLG, Live Tables 244 and 104). Owner-occupation is declining and private enterprise is no longer delivering for that market. Trends suggest that building more homes will not result in more people owning their own homes; rather, it will lead to more homes/assets in the hands of investors. The industry is clear that *buy to let* has 'played an important role in the traditional build to sell model': 'BTL investors have been making up an average of 50% to 60% of sales in London or 30% outside London' (British Property Federation, 2017: 7). But this market is threatened by increased tax liabilities for landlords and increased restrictions on mortgage lending since the 2008 GFC. For that reason, the big companies have been exploring the potential of '*build to rent*' as an 'additional sales outlet from the build to sell model' (British

Property Federation, 2017: 7). Private enterprise hopes to substitute individual investors with larger investors backed by institutional capital. Although government continues to support the aspiration towards owner-occupation, and is 'not prepared to stand by when people who want to get on the housing ladder can't do so' (*The Guardian*, 2015c), volume producers – Britain's largest 25 housebuilders – are not motivated to deliver against that aspiration. They are in the business of building houses and making money – with much of that money coming from investors, who rent houses to those who need them. For this reason, owner-occupation is declining and private renting in increasing. *Build to rent* promises to professionalise private renting, eradicating many of the problems associated with amateur landlordism. But it is also a means for big companies to maintain their market dominance – limiting the available space for alternative providers and different housing models and types.

The headline 80:20 split, between private/non-private production and with the former dominated by *build to sell*, reveals a lack of diversity – or plurality – in housing production. There has been a recent focus in policy debate on the decline of smaller and medium-sized housebuilders. In 1977, small housebuilders (companies building between 1 and 100 units each year) were responsible for 45% of private sector housing output, falling to just over 10% in 2015 (HBF, 2017: 15). Between 1988 and 2015, the number of small housebuilders fell by more than 80%. The number of medium-sized housebuilders (delivering between 101 and 2,000 units each year) reduced by just over 53%. During the same period, the number of big housebuilders grew by nearly 8% (HBF, 2017: 16). A number of factors contributed to this rescaling of the industry. From the point of view of the Home Builders Federation, important changes in the planning system in the 1990s 'tipped the balance of control' away from entrepreneurial housebuilders to local planning authorities (HBF, 2017: 7). Then, a decade later, the GFC resulted in a rationing of development finance which hit smaller housebuilders hardest. More generally, the planning system, with its various negotiations, agreements and uncertainties, generates proportionally bigger risks for smaller companies. Larger companies are better able to cope with those risks and bear the costs. Research by de Magalhaes et al (2018) reported the view that the one big scheme that goes ahead covers the costs of several others that fail to get off the ground. Smaller companies, with less working capital, are unable to 'play the odds' in this way and, according to the HBF, need the cushion of a more supportive planning process: less committee oversight on smaller sites, in-principle permission on some of these sites, and even technical support from planning authorities to help smaller companies get started (HBF, 2017: 9).

The volume housebuilding industry, which dominates housing production in the UK, works with economies of scale. It is generally looking to develop larger sites, or at least not the very small sites where just a handful of new homes will be built. If small housebuilders, often building *to contract* rather than speculatively, are absent from the market then this will impact on both total housing output and the contribution of other housing models to wider access. The HBF (2017: 25) argues that 'if the SMEs that have disappeared since 2007 were replaced and were able to maintain supply at the same annual rate as their current contemporaries, we could expect to see an additional 25,000 homes produced each year'. Relative to the output required to 'flatten the market' (as discussed above), this is perhaps small beer, but the contribution of a more mixed model of housing delivery should not be judged solely in terms of supply quantum. Satsangi et al (2010: 114) have observed that the lack of smaller housebuilders in many rural areas is a key impediment to housing production and access. They have a role to play in working with others on alternative production models, including self-build and the delivery of housing through community land trusts.

'Rebuilding plurality' in housing production – a term used by the HBF (2017: 25) – extends to non-market models that engage with market providers, including small and medium-sized enterprises (SMEs). In response to manifestations of the housing crisis in various parts of the world, different authors and various bodies have advanced solutions that seek to circumvent standard land market processes or turn the consumers of housing into producers. These include community-based housing solutions built on 'land trust' models that emphasise 'resale restrictions used to preserve housing use for the [trusts'] target clientele, and an approach to citizen governance that privileges local communities' (Moore and McKee, 2012: 280). As their name suggests, land trusts acquire and take control of land in perpetuity, retaining it for community use and either granting leases to 'target clientele' or renting out homes. Communities or individuals may build homes themselves or work with private SMEs (Benson and Hamiduddin, 2017). They often aim to halt the trading in land that bids up the value of houses built on it. By retaining control of that land, and by being constituted as not-for-profit bodies, they may be able to regulate the onwards sale of leases, fixing sale prices to local incomes rather than allowing properties to be traded freely in the open market. In that way, they retain a supply of 'affordable homes' in perpetuity. All such innovations seek to overcome, at least locally, the structural challenges that are the main focus of this book, and as such might be viewed as surface interventions – extremely difficult to upscale and mainstream.

However, the proposition that marketised production and *build to sell* has narrowed the scope of housing solutions, limiting overall supply and local access, is a persuasive one and viewed by business and community interests alike as complicit in the broader housing crisis.

Proposition 5

The tax treatment of housing is hindering supply (for example, VAT on conversion), impeding market function (for example, stamp duty adding upfront costs on purchase) and driving rising demand for housing over other assets (for example, removal of Schedule A tax in the past, application of capital gains tax and inheritance tax, and the structure of council tax), with implications for the wider economy.

The tax system – alongside broader fiscal governance, extending to monetary policy and regulation affecting the financial sector – affects the housing system in three broad ways: it may assist or impede the supply of housing; it may affect market function through the setting of transaction costs; and it will make housing a more or less attractive asset class. In short, tax impacts on supply, trading and the pattern of demand and consumption.

The proposition briefly explored in this section is that various tax liabilities affecting housing in England *are* in fact impeding supply, 'gumming up the housing market' (Whitehead, 2017) and attracting capital investment into housing.

Twenty years ago the Urban Task Force, in its report *Towards an Urban Renaissance*, raised the issue of harmonising VAT on new-build and residential conversions (Urban Task Force, 1998). Tax on the latter was viewed as a brake on increasing housing supply through conversions, extensions and renovations that might make an added contribution to net supply, especially in some urban areas. The charging of VAT on such projects has been described by Barker (2014: 64) as a 'big anomaly'. A zero rate of VAT on 'renovations' (particularly bigger projects) 'would provide an incentive to extend the present stock so that areas would tend to become denser in terms of population per hectare' (Barker, 2014: 64). VAT also affects self-build projects and is changed at a rate of 20%. The rules critiqued by the Urban Task Force remain largely unchanged, although in some circumstances, relief is available on VAT payments. The DIY Housebuilders' Scheme allows

VAT to be reclaimed for building a new house, converting a building into a dwelling and bringing a dwelling that has not been lived in for at least a decade back into residential use. VAT on the materials used in the project, which is currently charged at 20%, is claimed back from HMRC. Labour and materials will carry a 0% rate for new build and a 5% rate for conversion. It is the move to a 0% rate on conversions that Barker has recently called for. These differentials may seem minor, but they add costs to increasing supply from subdivision in already built-up areas, decrease the likelihood of some empty homes being brought back into residential use, and present would-be self-builders with upfront costs that can only be recovered after expenditure has been incurred and by presenting claims to HMRC.

There are, of course, other taxes on supply which affect companies in the business of preparing land for development or building homes. Private enterprise can expect to be taxed on the profits it generates, but costs associated with land remediation can be set against corporation tax. Land Remediation Relief (LRR) can be claimed by landowners, developers and loss-making companies involved in land remediation (the latter can receive a tax credit). LRR was introduced in 2001 and aimed to bring former industrial land back into effective use. More recently, Derelict Land Relief (introduced by the Finance Act 2009) can also be claimed for remediation on priority sites listed on the National Land Use Database (NLUD). In short, the level of relief (from tax liability) is proportionally greater for commercial companies engaged in large projects on previously developed land. Small projects, sometimes by self-builders, may incur proportionally more tax. This may impede the goal of 'rebuilding plurality' in housing production, with VAT rules in particular working against small schemes, potentially undertaken by non-commercial entities such as community land trusts.

Taxes affecting supply and construction are perhaps less well known than taxes on ownership and trading, which shape patterns of housing consumption. Principal taxes on consumption in the UK are as follows: stamp duty payable on acquisition, calculated as a percentage of purchase price; regular council tax payable to the local authority in which a property is located; capital gains tax on homes not occupied as a primary residence; and 'inheritance' tax payable against an estate on death. The capital switch into fixed assets has been supported by the tax treatment of residential property in the UK and resulted in a fiscal conundrum, whereby taxes ease access into housing for some but bar the way for others (see Barker, 2014: 60–62). Owner-occupiers and investors derive relative tax advantage from owning land and property, capturing in-kind (imputed) or actual rent and losing relatively little of that rent through tax liability – with investors often setting up (special purpose vehicle) limited companies for the purpose of reducing that liability. For that reason, land and land tax has dominated some recent analyses of the housing crisis, which have ended with calls to reintroduce land value tax (akin to the Schedule A tax abolished in 1963) and reinstate capital gains tax for owner-occupiers on their primary residences (abolished in 1965). This would have the effect of shifting tax liability away from earned to unearned income – taxing land and property-based wealth rather than work – and thereby distribute the wealth concentrated in property more broadly, via the tax system. Returning to the present system, the following forms of tax are viewed as problematic.

First, stamp duty: much has been written on the logic of stamp duty (see, for example, Andrew et al, 2003). It was, until 2015, a 'slab tax' payable at different rates at different price thresholds. At the low end of the market, governments have shown occasional concern for the impact of stamp duty on first-time buyers, increasing the price threshold at which the lowest rate (1% of purchase value) is payable and removing the duty altogether for first-time buyers purchasing homes under a certain value. The presented goal has been to ease entry into homeownership. Such moves, however, add to house price inflation and to the cost crisis: it was noted above that rates of homeownership have declined rapidly during the last decade. Further up the 'property ladder', stamp duty can act as a disincentive to (or simply prevent) trading up. This has been illustrated in recent work by Scanlon et al (2017b: 2), who argue that stamp duty contributes to England's 'dysfunctional housing market' by weakening housing market transaction and preventing both housing access and a better distribution of housing through downsizing. A survey by the authors showed that stamp duty added considerably to the cost incurred by older homeowners wishing to move to smaller properties, causing them to stay put. This has the effect of reducing the numbers of larger homes available to families in the second-hand market. More generally, stamp duty presents an enormous transaction cost to would-be movers, especially in London (see Figure 4.7).

When stamp duty was a slab tax (payable at a flat rate depending on sale price), this caused price distortion in the middle bands as vendors and buyers 'shared' the liability through the former agreeing a sale price below the nearest threshold (this caused a bunching of prices at that threshold rather than a smooth gradation – Barker, 2014: 59). This no longer happens. The main concerns today relate to the impact on trading, on achieving a better distribution of housing

Figure 4.7: SDLT on median priced home as a percentage of median gross full-time earnings, England and London, 1999–2016

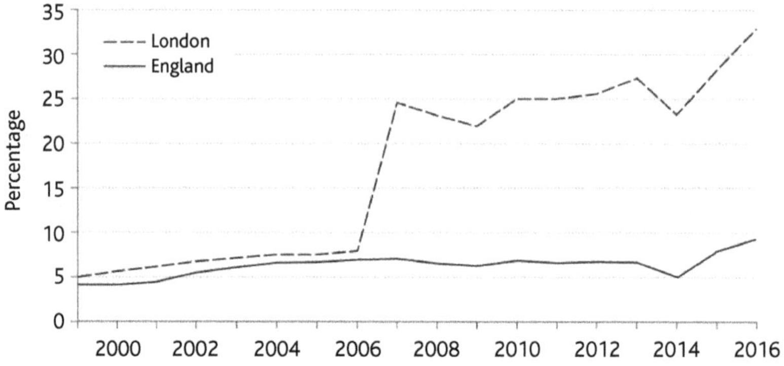

Source: Scanlon et al, 2017b: 7; drawing on statistics from ONS

resource (Scanlon et al, 2017b: 26) and on general household and labour mobility (Scanlon et al, 2017b: 31; Edwards, 2015: 35). These and related problems have led Bowie (2017: 165) to conclude that 'stamp duty on the purchase of residential property should be replaced by a tax on the capital gain on land and property on disposal'. The problems associated with stamp duty seem to give weight to the case for looking again at capital gains. However, for new-build property, stamp duty is part of government's early cost recovery for investment in key infrastructure, including schools, healthcare and so on. Whether the future annual tax take from capital gains on *all* residential property would be roughly equal to the current total revenues from stamp duty is a question that I return to in Chapter 6.

Second, capital gains tax: this tax (on rising property value, as unearned income) is not charged on a primary residence. Barker (2014: 60) argues that it could be charged, and perhaps should be, bringing 'the taxation of housing into line with other assets' and discouraging 'over-investment in housing'. Levying capital gains tax on main homes would be justified as recompense for the public investments – in good schools and transport infrastructure – that lift prices above the level achieved through householder improvements. But in the absence of capital gains tax, housing remains an almost perfect investment vehicle: 'trading up' to a larger home is as much about securing a 'bigger pot' for untaxed gains as it is about securing additional space for a growing family (though it was shown above that stamp duty may impede trading up). However, proponents of extending capital gains tax in this way concede concerns over the likely impact on household mobility. The tax could become another brake on the mobility of labour (besides its wider effects on consumer confidence). For this reason, Barker (2014: 61) proposes that accumulated liabilities could be rolled into a higher rate of inheritance tax.

But such a move would swim against the tide of public expectation. Successive governments have raised the level at which inheritance tax becomes payable, while no action has been taken to 'regulate the trust-like devices used to circumvent inheritance tax' (Edwards, 2015: 34). Barker's proposal is that capital gains tax on a lifetime of property trade-ups would be payable (or 'subtracted') from a person's estate and form part of the inheritance tax liability, decreasing the 'incentive to hold housing assets for investment' (Barker, 2014: 62). Hence, inheritance tax would become a vehicle for taxing capital gains while softening the impact on mobility and consumer confidence. Edwards (2015: 35) argues that it should also switch from being a 'charge on estates to being a charge on those who inherit', increasing revenue generated and more widely disbursing intergenerational wealth. These debates are important, but the system as it stands – a zero rate of capital gains for owner occupiers, opportunities to reduce liability through limited company structures for buy to let investors, and no effective land value tax – continues to shape patterns of housing consumption.

Council tax is the third major area of concern. The current banding system (linking property values to annual liability) is based on a valuation exercise undertaken nationwide on 1 April 1991. In the 27 years since that exercise, the geography of house prices has altered dramatically: today, 'those living in local authorities where house prices have been relatively weak – often poorer areas – tend to be overtaxed [and] those in high-value properties are undertaxed due to the width of the highest council tax band' (Barker, 2014: 65). So the first problem with the tax is that poorer households pay, proportionally, much more than wealthier ones. Once the highest band is reached ('H' for a property valued at £320,000 or more in 1991) the liability is fixed and does not change irrespective of a property's current value. The owners of high-end property in central London – including homes worth many millions of pounds – will pay the same as the occupant of a modest terraced house in many suburban parts of the city. At the root of the council tax question is uncertainty over what the tax is and what it seeks to achieve. As well as being a charge for local services (perhaps justifying its relatively 'flat' structure), it is also a 'proxy for a land value tax on the area a dwelling occupies' and 'a substitute for VAT on the consumption of housing services' (Barker, 2014: 66). But to perform these last two tasks well, council tax would need to link to land prices and imputed rents. If it does not then some housing will remain grossly under-taxed, but if it does (and there is an annual re-evaluation of tax liability based on land prices and rents) then council tax would become an inherently unstable means of funding local services, being suddenly coupled to market volatility. Barker (2014: 66–8) sets out a number of reform options; but the point here is that council tax, as currently constituted, is a poor substitute for a land value or property tax and represents one of the key ways in which housing investment is under-taxed and hence incentivised (see also Muellbauer, 2005).

The treatment given to tax in this section has, first, been very broad and, second, focused mainly on the way that liabilities affect owner-occupiers. More could have been said on second homes and income from *buy to let*. Equally, the impact of capital gains on the consumption of investment property has been mentioned only in passing: besides the use of limited companies for acquiring and holding property, there are various ways to reduce liability through renting out homes (claiming 'renting allowance'), refurbishing property to increase capital value (and offsetting tax with claimable expenditure) or 'flipping' between first and second homes to avoid capital gains altogether (Paris, 2010). But the general 'proposition' is, I think, illustrated by this brief examination of a selection of taxes: these present barriers to greater diversity in housing production 'gum up' the market and work against a better distribution, and generally add to the attraction of holding housing as asset.

Proposition 6

Increased credit supply and money creation (achieved through financial deregulation) has been part of an economic strategy designed to activate new housing demand and consumption in support of the 'productive economy' and also the service-based economy (particularly financial services). This has had the effect of pumping new money/capital into the available housing supply and pushing prices out of the reach of households on average incomes – and even higher earners in some areas.

The sixth proposition was explored in some detail in the last chapter: hence its coverage here has been pared back. Debt is a source of financial income and profit – it is a tradeable commodity. It is therefore in the interests of banks to advance loans (to supply credit and, in doing so, create money), which thereafter provide a source of income, or which can be sold on in order to limit the bank's exposure to risk (that risk is passed to investors, who accept the risk in return for fixed income). There are two sources of demand for debt: from homebuyers in the primary mortgage market and from investors in the secondary mortgage market. Deregulated banks (see Wainwright, 2009) respond to that demand by creating money through the act of advancing loans, to an aggregate value greater than the balance of deposits held. Hence, fictional capital (Harvey, 1978) is created and the 'value' of property is set not by the homebuyer's estimate of utility, but by the bank's estimate of the value of the debt in the secondary mortgage market. Where there is no secondary mortgage market – and no securitisation of debt – property values will still be set by money supply and the estimate of profit from advancing a loan rather than banks choosing to minimise risk. Mortgages (debt) are a source of profit, hence the practice – especially in the run-up to the GFC – of encouraging borrowers with good credit ratings to borrow many multiples of their household earnings. When money is pumped into housing in this way, prices tend to react quickly. It was noted in Chapter 3, for example, that in September 1971, the Bank of England cut direct controls on lending through the Competition and Credit Control policy. This changed the relationship between earnings and borrowing potential: it essentially (and temporarily) increased money supply and prompted a rapid rise in house prices – 37% in 1972 and 32% in 1973.

The relationship between credit/money and property prices has been highlighted recently by Keen (2018) in a blog post preceding a yet-to-be-published technical paper. 'Banks', he argues, have been allowed by governments to 'create money and inflate house prices'. Moreover, 'the demand side of the housing market has one main factor: new mortgages created by the banks. *Monetary demand* for housing is therefore predominantly mortgage credit: the annual increase in mortgage debt'. Keen shows that when mortgage credit rises, so do house prices. The same point is made by Ryan-Collins et al, but linked to housing supply:

> a major driving force in UK house price increases in the last thirty years has been a relatively elastic supply of credit meeting a fixed supply of land along with increased speculative demand for home-ownership. Without the existence of a credit- and money-creating banking system, it is impossible to envisage how such huge increases in prices would have been possible given the slower pace of income growth. (Ryan-Collins et al, 2017: 117)

Keen (2018) illustrates the coupling of house price change to changes in aggregate household credit (because 'mortgage debt data isn't systematically collected'). His depiction of this relationship is shown in Figure 4.8.

Ryan-Collins et al (2017: 117; citing Goodhart and Hoffman, 2008), however, offer some words of warning: 'correlation is not causation and it is likely that rising house prices, potentially driven by other factors, lead to an increase in demand for mortgage credit, which itself helps to drive up house prices'. Credit supply (and money creation) is just one of the determinants of price (see Meen, 2011), but increased elasticity in its supply since the 'reregulation' of the 1980s has significantly magnified its role in price-setting. This, at least, is the core of this increasingly popular proposition. Indeed, the catastrophe of the 2008 GFC has focused attention on credit supply, underpinned by financial instruments, including the repackaging of bank debt. Analyses of the GFC regularly draw attention to its anchoring in subprime lending (see for example, Keen, 2017) and the propensity of banks, ahead of market failure, to pay less attention to the asset on which loans are secured *and* the capacity of borrowers to service debt. Regulators – including the Bank of England – keep a close eye on mortgage lending and household debt. If it runs too far ahead of available housing supply

Figure 4.8: UK house price change and household credit change, 1970–2018

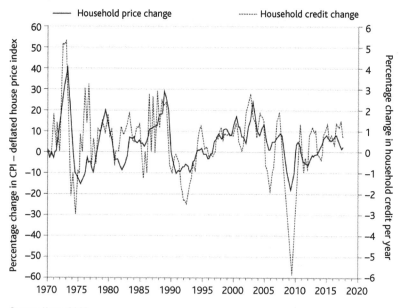

Source: Keen, 2018

then lending may need to be reined in. The reaction of politicians has traditionally been that credit growth is part of a healthy economy and will support the expansion of home ownership: problems in the housing market (for example, stretched affordability ratios relative to earnings) are down to suppressed supply. But as observed earlier in this chapter, a combination of new housebuilding (even if the rate is judged inadequate) and credit supply has not propelled English households into homeownership. More than one million new homes were delivered by private enterprise in the ten years to 2016. The number of homeowners fell by 31,000 during the same period. Between 50% and 60% of mortgage loan advances have gone to *buy-to-let* investors in London in recent years – and 30% elsewhere. Credit is playing an important role in the housing market, driving price inflation and also helping to steer the market away from owner-occupation.

Proposition 7

Returning to Proposition 1, above, housebuilding responds to money (credit) supply and not simply to housing need. The housing crisis is a disequilibrium between the supply of money and the supply of the housing asset. For those in need, this leads to declining affordability and crisis of access. But at the centre of this is the intentional refunction of the relationship between housing and the economy. This draws in overseas buyers (Proposition 2), privileges the private sector (Proposition 3) and owner-occupation (Proposition 4), functions on the basis of privileged tax treatment (Proposition 5) and is underpinned by the supply of credit/debt (Proposition 6).

The final proposition, and the conclusion to this chapter, is that all the above is linked. These are not separate pathways but parts of a complex system that generates the housing *cost crisis* that is evident not only in England but in different parts of the world: where growing reliance on private enterprise to build houses meets reduced bureaucratic provision, where credit supplied by a globalised banking system exceeds the realistic supply of homes, and where investors are invited to provide *market support* for the rising prices on which public finances depend. What does all this mean? It means that the unbroken trajectory over the last 30 years has been towards greater housing inequality, measured in terms of access to space and falling rates of owner-occupation. The recent surge in international and domestic investment has done nothing to reverse that trend. Investment in the form of production finance for speculative residential schemes may help to support 'affordable housing' procured through planning gain, but the amount and the actual affordability of that housing appears inadequate, given the widening gap between housing costs and workplace earnings.

Some of the recent studies reviewed in this chapter point to the possibility of slowing the movement of wealth into housing through incremental changes to taxation – for example, by introducing capital gains liability on the onward sale of primary residences, payable on 'final transaction' from the estate of deceased owners, or by reform of council tax; or through reform of bank regulation and lending rules, reconnecting loans to deposits held. But such moves would represent a significant reversal of decades-old support for homeownership, which has more recently become support for house price inflation without any attendant rise in owner-occupation. It is also the case that, as recent history shows, those encountering the most acute housing need are unlikely to benefit from the recession likely to accompany a fall in house prices. And even if recession could be avoided, slow and gradual deflation of the housing bubble would not bring fast relief for households currently locked out of the market.

The problem with particular formulations is that they attract adherents – those who, for whatever reason (politics or pragmatism), see an easy link between explanation and action. The purpose of Chapter 2 was to illustrate some of the complexity of factors underpinning housing outcomes, made all the more complex by those outcomes gestating in a contested political space. Most analyses embrace that complexity, searching for answers across different areas of public policy (planning, tax and financial regulation); though, ultimately, a chief villain is identified and a broad solution advanced: build more homes (generally or return to council building), reset the tax framework, prioritise the needs of domestic consumers over foreign ones, rein in the banks and so on. I will engage in this sort of big button pressing towards the end of the this book. But making housing more affordable (moving from commodification to re-communalisation) will not be the primary objective of systemic change. Systemic change, by definition, has broader goals – of which reduced housing costs and increased access will be an important side effect. The systemic change required in England relates to the economy and the basis of economic growth, which is currently underpinning critical inequalities and challenges to social cohesion – and also risking future prosperity.

5

Whose housing crisis?

The picture presented in Chapter 1 was of housing stress primarily affecting *generation rent* – young people, with no prior history of property ownership, unable to buy homes and stranded long term in the private rented sector. The plight of generation rent is a regular focus for the British press – aspiring homebuyers locked out of the property-owning benefits afforded their parents only a generation ago. Is the housing crisis theirs alone? Is the solution a matter of simply giving them a leg-up into homeownership, as the government regularly tries to do (or so it appears) through various market access supports? Those supports, however, operate at the fringe of the housing market. Families and individuals with some capital and good incomes are encouraged, by cuts in stamp duty or the promise of a 20% discount on a starter home, to make that final stretch to homeownership. This solution works for a few but the overall impact of such market supports is simply to smooth the path of additional wealth into housing – and, in aggregate, the proportion of homeowners in England has been declining rapidly. When the chancellor removed stamp duty for first-time buyers on homes costing less than £300,000 in November 2017, the Office for Budget Responsibility had already predicted that such a move would increase house prices by 0.3% within a year, offsetting much of the stamp duty saving available to those buyers. The chancellor's objective was, again, to keep house prices on their upward track, following the stumbling effect of his predecessor's hike in stamp duty on second homes and adjustments to the rate of tax relief available to the owners of *buy-to-let* properties, not to mention Brexit. Ahead of further negotiations on the UK's future trading relationship with the European Union, the objective was to support the economy through what was likely to be a turbulent period – and what better way to do so than to facilitate further investment in housing?

Although a clear political target, generation rent was never going to greatly benefit from this easing of transaction tax. The real beneficiary was the market and existing homeowners. So is everything good for existing owners? In answer to the question 'whose housing crisis?', is there a straightforward dichotomy between those with and without the ownership of private housing – a simple landed and landless division, perpetuating the range of outcomes suggested in Chapter 1, between mild inconvenience and abject poverty? In other words, is the increased concentration of wealth in housing broadly a good thing, only creating hardship at the fringes?

Investors and existing homeowners seem to be doing well. They have seen the equity in their property steadily grow over a number of years. Housing is their *wealth machine*, providing them and their families with security. As mortgages are slowly repaid, their disposable income rises – providing money for luxury items, for holidays, and also the means to fund their children's education and meet their own retirement needs. The advantages they enjoy are captured in the idea of 'domestic property classes' (Saunders, 1978, 1984). In 1984, Saunders wrote that 'the significance of domestic property ownership for the distribution of wealth, the structuration of classes and the mobilization of political conflicts has in recent years been the subject of widespread academic debate and political argument' (1984: 202). Saunders' particular concern was for how private ownership might be 'reconciled with socialist principles of equity and collectivism' (p. 202) in the context of the sale of council homes to sitting tenants, which had begun a few years before. While he questioned the extent to which the 'structuration of classes' is dependent on the ownership of housing, it seems reasonable to argue that one's outlook is shaped by market position – and the journey taken to reach that position. Does the new homeowner, who has struggled and saved to get a foothold on the first rung of the housing ladder want house price inflation to slow or flatten? The answer is likely to be no, for two reasons. First, they are likely to have accessed homeownership with a significant loan advance and may have incurred significant transaction costs (stamp duty, agents' and conveyancing fees). They now need to recover the transaction costs (within a fixed number of years so they are able to move again, should they need to) and also feel confident that the purchase was worth it: that ultimately the home will be worth more than the principal plus interest repayments on the mortgage. Second, their expectations of homeownership are broader than having a place to live: this home, or another that they purchase as they climb the ladder, will be an asset against which to borrow for life's other expenses: those already listed above. I think we can therefore forgive homeowners for wanting to see steady rises in house prices and for viewing as unacceptable the idea that the capital gain in the value of their home should be taxed. Policies aimed at supporting homeownership are popular among this property class: that others will come to share in the things they enjoy, and that their own wealth will grow (as 'society' invests in housing), are comforting ideas, especially when there is rising awareness of the plight of generation rent. There are challenges, however, in reconciling this view of the housing crisis with the deep structural transformations described in this book, and also with trend data on homeownership and affordability. The cost crisis, with house prices and rents racing far ahead of earnings, and with demand for housing and loan advances being dominated by investors, could suggest that we are heading into much more turbulent waters.

In this chapter, I want to offer two concluding perspectives on the housing crisis. The first perspective is that the crisis affects the fringes of society: those struggling to house themselves or who are locked out of the market and reliant on a diminishing pool of state support. This is the manageable crisis with clear boundaries, which can be tackled within the current political economy. Governments choose to focus attention on the specific groups (of voters) enduring this kind of hardship and, depending on the size of those groups, will take small or large steps to remedy or alleviate that hardship within the life of a single parliament. Centre and centre-right governments have tended, over the last 40 years, to prioritise market entry (through the *right to buy*, *help to buy* and different forms of intermediate tenure 'affordable housing' that give voters access to homeownership). Politicians on the left (there have been no left-leaning governments during the same period) point to the need to regrow state involvement in housing: to build council housing again. This perspective, with its own political branches, identifies its fringe and sets out what might be done to help its priority groups. The second perspective is that the housing crisis (being the tip of an enormous iceberg) merely expresses an economic imbalance and a level of *inequality* – grounded in the distribution of housing wealth and the capture of land rent – that is now undermining the foundations of Western civilisation, no less. This is the crisis without clear boundaries: the *wicked problem* that cannot be addressed while the current political economy is preserved. It is rooted in the economic transition tracked in Chapter 3 and signals a level of inequality and social stratification that now poses a clear and present danger not only to future prosperity but to the existing social order, and the underlying values, of those societies it afflicts.

Housing as a fringe concern

For those who view the housing crisis as having a bounded effect on specific social groups or property classes – for example, the young (without significant parental support and no prior history of home ownership), or other lower-income groups dependent on state support – problem-definition is straightforward. The system has not met their needs and requires adjustment. That is not to say that the crisis is not viewed as having pervasive, and hugely damaging, characteristics. Housing is seen as linking to many other things: to education, social mobility, jobs and life chances. It is a crisis felt acutely by one or more groups, but which also weakens the economic and social fabric, affecting labour supply and causing frustration and disillusionment. Intergenerational conflict may become a challenge, as may the concentration of wealth in fewer hands as inheritance plays its part in shaping future patterns and levels of inequality. But still, all is rectifiable with the right interventions.

Ways in which different groups are affected by housing stress are recounted by Minton (2017). She paints a picture of a stratified crisis. The worst-off households and individuals endure Victorian standards of overcrowding and slum conditions in the private rented sector, accessing rooms to let not through regulated agents but by responding to advertisements in newsagents' windows:

> one in particular stood out, offering a room share for four people for £160 a month, effectively a bed space in what may or may not be legal accommodation. Renting bed spaces, I had already heard from a number of sources, is becoming a more common way of renting, with bunkbeds visible in the front rooms of nearby terraces.
> (Minton, 2017: 97)

Investigations with housing officers, many of whom had witnessed first-hand some of the worst cases of room-cramming and 'rent to rent' practice in London, revealed cases of half a dozen people crowded into single rooms. The 'rent to rent' phenomenon ranges from simple illegal subletting, to criminal gangs renting entire houses and then filling them with bunkbeds before subletting bed spaces to individuals. In that way, modest family homes can be filled with dozens of occupants – reaching levels of overcrowding not seen in the city for more than a hundred years. Minton also focuses on the 'beds in sheds' phenomenon: 'unauthorised dwellings located in rear gardens' (2017: 98). Citing a report commissioned by a member of the London Assembly, the *Evening Standard* claimed in December 2017 that there are now 9,000 'beds in sheds' across London (Evening Standard, 2017). Criminal exploitation combines with spiralling land and housing costs to produce these most extreme outcomes.

Minton (2017: 102–3) points out that, today, '11 million people in Britain rent privately in an overlapping series of submarkets ranging from the poor conditions and slum housing at the bottom end to student accommodation, micro "pocket living" flats, apartments for professionals and luxury housing at the top'. Generation rent is often thought to comprise not those households in the very first submarket, but rather the 'third of private renters' who are aspiring owners (Minton, 2017: 103). A generation ago, the same group – on similar incomes and with the same aspirations – *were* owners. Minton recounts the situations and reflections of a number of individuals broadly falling into this group. One was said to 'earn enough to get a mortgage but, because rents are so high, not enough to save for the 20–30 percent deposit required' (p. 106). Their feelings on this were presented as typical, captured in the following quote: "The common thread for people my age is that we don't own our own homes and potentially we never will." The crisis is attributable to 'structural neglect', to the '*buy to let* boom' and an 'unregulated market'. The solution lies in 'a different way of looking at property' (p. 106).

The idea that the housing crisis is experienced by three distinct 'thirds' is a useful one. Towards the end of the opening chapter, I suggested a continuum of housing stress, from mild inconvenience to abject poverty – with a top, middle and bottom. The 'thirds' that Minton flags – drawing on the comments of the director of the lobby group 'Generation Rent' – are those households in slum housing (including 'rent to rent' or 'beds in sheds'), those *content to rent* but who want better quality homes (and more secure tenancies), and those who aspire to own their own homes but who are unable to take their first steps onto the housing ladder. If the housing crisis is bounded in this way (*bounded* in the sense that it only affects those who are badly or inadequately housed relative to aspiration) then corresponding solutions – the usual ones – seem to jump out: subsidised affordable homes, a professionalised rental sector and policies to support ownership.

That housing (affordability and access) is a bounded and narrowly defined issue is captured by the *housing ladder* metaphor. This metaphor, regularly invoked by politicians, views generation rent as a growing constituency of voters who are unable to get a foothold on the first rung of that ladder. They are unable to begin their *housing careers*: a career that will involve, over time, trading upwards and growing their store of equity – which can one day be released, for retirement, or to pay for late-life care. The first rung provides a focus for politicians (and for proponents of narrow, incremental action) because aspiring first-time buyers are a growing political constituency and also because getting people onto that rung is thought, in some quarters, to be critical to facilitating movement/trading higher up the ladder (it ensures a 'functioning' and 'healthy' market – one that is not 'broken'). That last point is debateable and was questioned in Chapter 3. If existing owners are levering more borrowing against the property they already own, and ploughing that money back into *buy to let* or investing in rental housing in other ways, then the market can continue to function without the same volume of first-time buyers. More recent generations are simply consigned to long-term renting, paying off the mortgages of the previous generation and eventually their children. Housing wealth becomes more concentrated and past (feudal) landed/ landless divisions are reconstituted for the twenty-first century. Even a narrow focus on the fate of generation rent points to more fundamental concerns, centred broadly on social inequality and intergenerational cohesion – and more particularly on basic questions of sustainability. Given the ongoing shift from state to asset-based welfare (which was meant to be an outcome of more broadly distributed wealth), how will generation rent pay for the education of its children (unless post-18 education is freely provided by the state), retire (and meet its housing costs) or fund social care in later life? The pursuit of concentrated wealth through the market rather than broadly distributed welfare is likely to leave a trail of unpaid bills, which will eventually need to be footed through higher taxation.

Housing as a fundamental concern

Housing is *not* a fundamental concern, but its affordability and accessibility signals a far deeper economic and social malaise. This is the opposing perspective, which is nevertheless only a short jump from the bounded view. It was noted above that housing is regularly viewed as a wealth or growth 'machine'. This is a downscaling of a more general perspective on cities: 'for those who count, the city is a growth machine, one that can increase aggregate rents and trap related wealth for those in the *right position* to benefit' (Logan and Molotch, 2010: 87). Some of those in the 'right position' were identified in Chapter 3, and include global investors and others who directly hold, and trade in, land and property. But the capture of rent is also the domain of domestic homeowners. If ownership of property recedes then wealth becomes more concentrated, with broader social implications. This is happening in England at the present time (see Dorling, 2014b: 114– 15). Following Christophers (2010: 106), 'rent does not constitute added value' and notional growth cannot indefinitely substitute for real growth. But whatever the foundation of growth, real or nominal, the unequal distribution of benefit raises both economic and moral questions. Friedman (2005: 436) believes strongly in the power of growth to deliver a better society: 'only with sustained economic growth, and the sense of confident progress that follows from the advance of living standards for *most* of its citizens, can even a great nation find the energy, the wherewithal, and most importantly the human attitudes that together sustain an open, tolerant, and democratic society'. Others have argued that growth is not central to achieving those things, and the planet cannot sustain growth dependence (see, for example, Daly, 1997; Jackson, 2009). But they agree that the broadest sharing of benefits, from growth or stasis, is important. Friedman relates a nation's 'economic experience' with a range of social and political outcomes. His hypothesis is that growth is associated with periods of 'movement *toward* openness, tolerance, mobility, fairness, democracy' and that periods of stagnation produce movement '*away from*' these things (Friedman, 2005: 110). His book explores this hypothesis in forensic detail – primarily by looking at episodes of growth and stagnation in the United States – and reaches the conclusion noted above: the former brings tolerance and happiness. But this must be real growth, reflected in rising earnings relative to costs. Inflation outpaced workplace earnings in the US during the 1970s and 1980s: 'by 1993 the median income of all American men working full time ... was 5 per cent less than it was in 1973' (Friedman, 2005: 198). Wage stagnation meant that 'home ownership rates ... declined throughout the 1980s' and 'working Americans who were young in the early 1970s saw little real change in their incomes over the next two decades of their careers. And by the early 1990s their children were having to start off, on average, far behind where they had started' (Friedman, 2005: 199). A very similar situation is being faced in England today: stagnating earnings and falling rates of home ownership. Many individuals' self-assessments of their economic and future wealth prospects are often bleak (see Minton, 2017). For the US in the 1990s, Friedman (2005: 199) associated the same situation with a marked slowing of 'movement towards opening American society, either domestically or with respect to outsiders'.

The closure observed by Friedman is attendant on declining confidence: a society with a predilection towards protection. Growth, broadly shared, is the means of avoiding this. But it has to be the right kind of growth: with basic costs, and future increases in those costs, not running ahead of earnings. For Friedman, the growth machine has to be kept switched on – explaining economies' search for new growth platforms and drivers under the capitalist mode of production. The refocusing on the built environment – and housing in particular – as a source of that growth presents numerous problems, not least the substitution of real with nominal growth, wage stagnation and the relative housing cost crisis. Indeed, the capital switch – previously described and tracked – has very fundamental implications for the housing system and its outcomes. It has brought two critical forces into play: the first is a financialised (or 'monetarised' – see Keen, 2018) demand for property consumption, which has ecological consequences; the second is property-based inequality that now underpins more pronounced social stratification (amplifying concerns raised by Saunders in 1984) and a descent into the unhappiness and social malaise described by Friedman.

Motesharrei et al (2014) have examined how the interplay of these forces may, in practice, ultimately produce more than moral consequences. They pose this fundamental question: 'can complex, advanced civilisations really collapse?' (Motesharrei et al, 2014: 90). The first part of their answer is that history has seen many 'rise-and-collapse cycles', not just in Europe but right across the 'old' and 'new' worlds. Rather than being rare, they are recurrent and widely distributed – and 'advanced, sophisticated, complex and creative' civilisations are as susceptible as any other (p. 91). Such collapses have a variety of triggers, from natural disaster to economic and social upheaval. But it is pointed out that civilisations that endured for hundreds of years often overcame single events and continued to thrive. It was only when they faced a particular set of circumstances, with a catastrophic aggregate effect, that their end came. The authors set out to explore and model those circumstances – to engage in 'thought experiments for the phenomenon of collapse'. The historical cases reveal two very significant factors that appear to have contributed to collapse: 'the stretching of resources due to the strain placed on the ecological carrying capacity' and 'the economic stratification of society into elites and masses' (p. 91). Using a 'predator–prey model', the researchers undertook a mathematical modelling exercise to explore the likelihood of societies with stretched resources and acute economic stratification finding equilibrium (and continuing) or going the same way as the Roman Empire.

Three sets of scenarios were examined. These involved an unequal society in which elites consume many times more resources than the rest, an egalitarian society without elites (and without big differentials in consumption), and an equitable society in which 'non-workers' and 'workers' have the same level of consumption (that is, no social stratification) (Motesharrei et al, 2014: 99–100). Regarding the first set of scenarios, the following comments are offered:

> The scenarios most closely reflecting the reality of our world today are [the unequal societies] where we introduced economic stratification. Under such conditions, we find that collapse is difficult to avoid, which helps to explain why economic stratification is one of the elements recurrently found in past collapsed societies ... elites eventually consume too much, resulting in a famine among commoners. (Motesharrei et al, 2014: 99)

This 'inequality-induced famine causes a loss of workers rather than a collapse of nature'. They are denied the resources they need to contribute to production. Elites allow this to happen because their

> buffer of wealth allows elites to continue 'business as usual' despite the impending catastrophe ... this buffer effect is further reinforced by the long, apparently sustainable trajectory prior to the beginning of the collapse. While some members of society might raise the alarm that the system is moving towards an impending collapse and therefore advocate structural changes to society in order to avoid it, elites and their supporters, who opposed making these changes, could point to the long sustainable trajectory 'so far' in support of doing nothing.
> (Motesharrei et al, 2014: 100)

Subsequent analysis of the trajectories of egalitarian and equitable societies is designed to draw attention to the sorts of structural changes that might be needed if these outcomes are to be avoided. Mathematical modelling does not convey what an 'inequality-induced famine' might look like, but it is likely to include declining productivity and wage stagnation, pushing all the things that the elites consume well out of reach of the commoners, before precipitating a collapse in the real economy. Motesharrei et al (2014) bring science to an area of debate – centred on inequality – that has seen many popular contributions in recent years: these include, notably, Piketty's *Capital in the Twenty-first Century* (2014), Wilkinson and Pickett's *The Spirit Level* (2010), Sayer's *Why We Can't Afford the Rich* (2015), and Dorling's *Inequality and the 1%* (2014b). All argue that the wealth of the rich – increasingly concentrated in and extracted from land and housing – amounts to the extraction of value created by others, and is unstainable.

While the fight against inequality might be viewed as a rallying call for the left (requiring market correction), even advocates of market liberalism see dangers in the unequal distribution of wealth and resources (see Friedman, 2005). There has been particular concern over social cohesion in some Western societies, especially intergenerational cohesion as wealth becomes more concentrated in the hands of older people, while younger generations are called upon to work longer to sustain public and workplace pensions, and more general welfare spending on late-life care. More broadly – and following the analyses of Friedman (2005) and Motesharrei et al (2014) – there remain concerns over the longer-term sustainability of Western prosperity, even if short-term measures can address the worst manifestations of inequality and weak social cohesion. In the remainder of this chapter, I focus on these three issues: inequality, social cohesion and prosperity. The purpose is to illustrate the importance of housing wealth and housing systems to the creation and alleviation of these critical challenges.

Inequality

The study of inequality is a crowded field and this book does not aim to contribute insights beyond those offered elsewhere. Sayer's (2015) provocation – 'why we can't afford the rich' – is a good starting point for thinking about the centrality of housing in 'wealth extraction' (and the production of rising inequality). For Sayer (2015), the rich are the extractors rather than the creators of wealth:

> Their wealth is mostly dependent ultimately on the production of goods and services by others and siphoned off through dividends, capital gains, interest and rent, and much of it is hidden in tax havens. ... Their consumption is excessive and wasteful and diverts resources away from the more needy and deserving. Their carbon footprints are grotesquely inflated and many have an interest in continued fossil fuel production, threatening the planet. (Sayer, 2015: 2)

The control of fixed assets – land and property – is critical to the extraction of wealth: 'what you get depends on what you have, and what you have determines what you need to do to get an income. If you have assets like land and buildings that others need, you can get rent. If you have spare money, you can get interest' (Sayer, 2015: 43–4). Over time, competition for assets (and the greater availability of bank credit to facilitate that competition) has caused a bidding-up of prices and rationing through the market. Available data from England show increased concentration of assets in the form of privately owned homes: *fewer* people control *more* of what is needed to derive asset-based income. In response to this predicament, a reversal of existing patterns of inequality might seem to depend on a different distribution of housing resource (which is the broad argument advanced by Dorling, 2014a). This supposes that patterns of wealth and relative poverty will continue to be underpinned by the private control of land and property, and therefore by the process of wealth extraction. This being the case (and there seems to be no prospect of radical change on the horizon), revamping the way in which ordinary households rent property, for example, will not dramatically alter high levels of income inequality.

One of the suggested pathways to the current housing crisis in England, set out in Chapter 4, is the overreliance on *build to sell*. In response to that overreliance, it has been proposed that institutional investment in *build to rent* could be a means of improving the experience of renting housing, in terms of its overall quality and the stability it offers households. Those who are 'content to rent' may derive some benefit from this model. But why are these households content to rent if their future wealth is tied to the control of assets? There are likely to be a mix of answers to this question: relating to life stage, to locational preference, to short-to-medium-term mobility needs (for example, chasing state school places), to personal income levels, and to the expectation of inheriting property and/or the ownership of property that they do not currently live in. This is conjecture: there are no data that I am aware of on higher-income renters' patterns of property ownership (or broader housing histories). But it seems certain that while housing retains a central role in generating wealth for its owners, models such as *build to rent* will not deliver against the expectations and aspirations of many people. Rather, they will sustain, and may further accentuate, inequality. While they may squeeze out some individual (*buy to let*) investors, they create new pathways into housing for big institutional investors – new ways to siphon off 'dividends, capital gains, interest and rent'.

Movement to a more mixed housing system – extending through *build to rent* to new forms of social housing – will only be part of a march towards greater income equality if coupled with a radically different approach to capturing and redirecting capital gains and rent.

A number of authors focused on questions of inequality support the introduction of improved systems of land value taxation. Dorling (2014a: 51) proposes the extension of 'current council tax bands up to band "z"' as part of a system of fairer land and property taxation. Bringing 'rent under democratic control' with the taxing of ground rent through a *land value tax* is also proposed by Sayer (2015). Private 'rent-seeking' is, for Sayer, absolutely central to patterns of inequality around the world: 'buying up land in Africa in anticipation of future commercial exploitation' has, for example, not benefited local groups but 'merely inflated share values' (2015: 42) for portfolio investors. Investment in *build to rent* in London, however, produces a different outcome: there is a benefit measured in housing quality, tenure stability and cost. There are gains for some households from this different form of investment-supported housing, delivered through private enterprise. Likewise, public housing – backed by a combination of bank loans, tax subsidy and local planning agreements – can be presented as a good outcome from the current system. Those with a vested interest in that system – who are 'in the right position to benefit' – will claim that it is the wealth (the value) that they create which is ploughed back into these essential public goods: nothing is possible without investment capital and the market/production support it provides. For that reason, investment and investors should be welcomed into the housing market and into the residential development sector (Scanlon et al, 2017a: 29). But that value has almost invariably been generated by the labour of others, extracted and only partially returned (the rest being siphoned off). That partial return by those who control land and property is central to the inequality crisis and the housing crisis therein.

Again, Sayer's distinction between wealth *creation* and wealth *extraction* is critical: if the rich are wealth creators, then the processes of housing production cannot be progressed without them. They are the providers of finance – the many millions of pounds often needed to assemble and remediate sites and get big residential schemes off the ground. But if, on the other hand, they are extractors – extracting rent and interest, which is 'parasitic' on the work of producers (Sayer, 2015: 42) –then those production processes can function perfectly well with less of the *private* finance derived from the *private* extraction of value, assuming that value has been retained through democratic control over rent. More broadly, income inequalities can be flattened by shifting the tax burden away from earned income (through income tax) to unearned income (through some form of land value tax). This could be achieved through the restoration of Schedule A income tax, which was abolished back in the 1960s (see Bowie, 2017: 167).

Control of land and property is core to the global challenge of inequality. It underpins the economic stratification introduced in the models built by Motesharrei et al (2014), in which unequal societies – characterised by 'grotesque consumption' on the one hand and resource 'famine' on the other – ultimately collapse under the weight of parasitic wealth extraction. Our relationship with housing is a big part of all of this, because among all the 'buildings that others need', homes are one of the most basic of human requirements.

Social cohesion

A more general concern arising from (or broadly related to) income inequality is social cohesion. The OECD (2011) says that social cohesion is produced by three critical components: the *inclusion* of individuals in society (their ability to participate and freedom from barriers to that participation); social *mobility* (individuals' capacity to get ahead through access to education, work – and subsequent rises in income/spending power – and because they are treated fairly and without prejudice); and *social capital* (a social state in which resources are shared, support is reciprocated and there is cooperation between groups, aimed at achieving some common public good). Embedded in that definition are many uncertainties, complexities and points of contention. There is a vast literature on social cohesion, and also on inclusion, mobility and social capital – which cannot be reviewed here. However, different aspects of housing-related inequality would seem to impinge on social cohesion. First, difficulty in accessing the right home in the right location is a potential barrier to inclusion; it may deprive individuals of important opportunities: employment, key services or access to the best or right schools for their children (laying the foundation, perhaps, for impeded social mobility later on). Second, because nominal growth (based on the value being extracted from property and reflected in rising house prices) is outstripping real growth and resulting in wage stagnation, workplace earnings are no longer a means, for many, of securing broader social mobility. Rather, mobility is achieved disproportionately by property owners – who often see the value of their homes exceed their incomes from other sources, who subsequently accumulate wealth, and who thereby extend their capacity to buy opportunities for themselves and their children. This is the feedback loop of inequality, magnified from one generation to the next. And third, the uneven distribution of housing is a threat to cooperation and reciprocity between social groups (that is, social capital), especially if older homeowners (acquiring their property at a very different price point in the market) benefit from the rising house prices that lock younger people out of the market, and those younger people work longer hours for stagnant wages – the victims of 'structural neglect'.

In light of population aging (and the increased burden this places on the taxpayer) among the baby boomer generation – many of whom are homeowners – and declining rates of owner-occupation and related social mobility among 'millennials', there has been a recent political and media focus on intergenerational cohesion in England and the rest of the UK. The reality of many older people voting to leave the European Union in the 2016 referendum, while the majority of younger people are said to have voted to remain, has brought this divide into even sharper focus. In 2005, Kotlikoff and Burns charted the 'coming generational storm': baby boomers in the US living longer and drawing social security, and 'the number of children coming of age and joining the workforce' not being 'nearly enough' (Kotlikoff and Burns, 2005: 3) to support rising social costs. Their answer to this dilemma was 'homeownership', which will 'reduce the impact of a decline in social security benefits and an increase in taxation' (p. 205). But this supposes that as the population gets older, homeownership – as a source of asset-based welfare – continues to grow. The housing cost crisis in England has produced a decline in homeownership (from nearly 68% in 2007 to 63% in 2017): older people still own their homes, but younger people are consigned to generation rent. England's own 'generational storm' is likely to be particularly pronounced given the combination of demographic and housing market drivers. Fifteen years ago, the BBC aired a number of future scenario 'drama documentaries'. One explored the prospect of intergenerational conflict: *If... the Generations Fall Out* imagined a future in which disgruntled twenty- to forty-somethings marched under banners proclaiming 'we pay – they play'. In 2004, when the programme aired, a lack of consistent saving and underperforming personal pensions had shifted welfare responsibility back to working-age taxpayers (BBC News, 2004). Since then, government has invested in promoting workplace pensions and national savings schemes. And, like other European countries, the UK is keeping the statutory retirement age – at which state pensions can be drawn – under review. But countering all of this has been the fall in the level of private homeownership and the worry, of many younger households, that they will still be renting into their 60s and 70s. For many, this would simply be unaffordable. People therefore envisage working until they die. That is, of course, not possible in most cases; the failure of asset-based welfare will result in higher taxation, with taxpayers footing the cost of private accommodation (through a future form of housing benefit) and then hospice care, unless family support becomes the norm. Having paid rent to landlords all their working lives, the state (that is, the taxpayer) will now step in to continue those payments for the next 20 or 30 years.

This supposes no future distribution of rent: no departure from the commodification of land and housing that has advanced so strongly in the twentieth century. It supposes the continued extraction of wealth through land rent, depriving an aging population of the means to live well into their retirement. Had that rent been brought under democratic control, the benefits of growth could have been shared more evenly. Politicians in England are aware of the intergenerational challenge, and the anger it – together with the housing crisis – is now provoking. In 2018, the Resolution Foundation, an independent think tank, published a report outlining the need for 'a new generational contract'. The old one – the status quo – had, according to the foundation's chairman, Lord Willetts, 'broken down' (BBC News, 2018d). The proposal to provide a cash payment of £10,000 to all 25-year-olds (a 'citizen's inheritance') – funded from a 'lifetime receipts tax' (payable above a tax allowance of £125,000), which would replace inheritance tax and generate projected revenues of £5 billion – achieved its aim of grabbing headlines. Other proposals, however, which recognised the centrality of housing to intergenerational fairness, sought more fundamental solutions to the wealth imbalance between the old and the young. Of the report's 15 housing-related proposals (Resolution Foundation, 2018: 218–19), four were concerned with the regulation of landlords and rent; one with housing benefit support; two with stamp duty and *help to buy* (risking the wrath of the Office for Budget Responsibility); four with planning, land auctions and housebuilding; one with *build to rent*; another with closing the housing market to foreign buyers in certain urban 'hotspots'; and two final proposals with capital gains (for owners of additional properties) and council tax. The tax proposals were the most interesting, in my view. The capital gains proposal – a time-limited tax amnesty for *buy-to-let* owners selling their properties to first-time buyers – was designed to provide amateur landlords (who are now faced with higher tax on rental income) with an exit route from the sector. It is also another way of supporting homeownership, if more second-hand property is released onto the market. The report also proposed the replacement of council tax with a progressive property tax, based on up-to-date values and with multiple bands.

Commenting on the proposals, Lord Willetts conceded that political parties were not expected 'to embrace them straightaway' (Resolution Foundation, 2018: 8). Rather, they were intended to trigger 'lively debates in the months and years ahead', from which would emerge new means to 'promote *asset ownership* for younger generations' (p. 8, emphasis added). The uneven distribution of assets was acknowledged as being central to the intergenerational crisis. Alleviation of that crisis will come, in part, from broadening asset (home) ownership and introducing some degree of democratic control over land rent through a progressive property tax. This would mean a bigger tax take from the asset-rich, to be redistributed through pensions, healthcare and the 'citizen's inheritance'. While the holding of land and property is viewed as a solution to intergenerational conflict, suppressing the extraction of real or imputed rent from those assets (through a combination of 'light-touch rent stabilisation', shrinking the *buy-to-let* sector, and property tax) would seem to restore some of the balance in the housing market that has been lost in recent years. Without that restoration, income inequality will grow while social cohesion will ebb away.

Wealth and prosperity

Questions of inequality and social cohesion align closely to concerns over wealth and prosperity, and whether wealth (the abundance of resource) will rise in the future and be more equitably shared, delivering prosperity (welfare, comfort, security and wellbeing) for the many. These concerns are inexorably linked to different perspectives on growth. Wilkinson and Pickett (2010: 226) cite Henry Wallich, a past governor of the US Central Reserve Bank, who observed in 1973 that 'wealth is a substitute for equality of income. So long as there is growth there is hope, and that makes large income differentials tolerable.' There are parallels here with Friedman's (2005) defence of growth, as a source of openness and tolerance. These outcomes are predicated on hope: the hope that growth will bring shared prosperity, that some future end state is worth present hardships. Wilkinson and Pickett contend that 'it is not simply that growth is a substitute for equality, it is that greater equality makes growth much less necessary' (2010: 226). In a steady-state economy, or one in which growth rates are extremely low, patterns of consumption are much flatter: there is a turn away from consumption driven by 'status competition'.

All the recent studies of inequality, cited earlier, converge on this point: a sustainable level of growth can deliver shared prosperity. It is the unequal extraction of wealth, and hyper-consumption, which necessitate unsustainable levels of growth-driven resource depletion. What does all this mean for the housing crisis in England? Control of land and housing facilitates multiple forms of hyper-consumption. The consumption of housing has two drivers: first, the need to gain control over land rents, as a source of income; and then, second, status competition. Future levels of wealth are therefore tied to the production and consumption of housing. This was illustrated in Chapter 3, which explored the housing sector's various connections to the economy and also the ways in which land rents are captured, directly through imputed and real rent, and also indirectly through the primary and secondary mortgage markets as interest and dividends. Public finances are also dependent, to some degree, on the production and consumption of housing. Housing has become a source of wealth creation, but not of broader prosperity.

Although there is unquestionably some degree of supply crisis in England, housing continues to be built, purchased and occupied. It was noted in the last chapter that private enterprise delivered just over one million homes in the ten years to 2016, all for private consumption. Yet during the same period, the number of owner-occupiers fell by more than 30,000. Is it possible to determine the proportion of England's private housing stock that forms part of multi-unit portfolios, and therefore judge the current concentration of wealth (achieved through the control of housing)? Roughly 60% of the UK's net wealth is in housing. Fifteen million households in England own the homes they live in (just under 63%). Another five million rent in the private sector, from small or large portfolio landlords. Analysis from the Council of Mortgage Lenders (2016), using HMRC figures, shows that there are roughly 1.75 million private landlords in the UK, who collectively earned £14.2 billion in rent in 2015. Just over 60% of those landlords rent out one property and another 30% have between two and four properties which they let. The remaining 10% have up to 24 properties. These figures on private renting include the 14% of private landlords operating as limited companies, usually for reasons of tax efficiency if they hold larger portfolios (Council of Mortgage Lenders, 2016). (These include those operating through offshore companies.) As well as owning properties that are regularly let to others (as their main home), a great many people also own second homes. The distinction between properties held as rental investments and those retained for personal use, perhaps as destinations for occasional holidays or weekend breaks, is not always clear (see Gallent et al, 2005). The Resolution Foundation (2017) has noted a 30% rise in the 'proportion of [UK] adults' owning multiple properties between 2000/02 and 2012/14. One in ten adults (5.2 million) now own more than one home. This is more than the total privately rented stock in England (and close to the total amount of rented homes across England, Scotland and Wales). Very approximately, a tenth of the population are multiple homeowners. They own homes that are not their full-time place of residence either within the UK or elsewhere in the world. Private landlords who rent out more than one home are responsible for about 2.9 million units; single unit landlords, another 1.1 million. These figures are all rough approximations from the Council of Mortgage Lenders 2016 survey. There is a big gap here with the total private renting figure from the MHCLG (Live Table 104, which also includes homes rented with a job or business) and the Resolution Foundation's (2017) general figure for adults owning multiple properties. But the following statement seems reasonable: while a *third* of households in England have no direct proprietorial interest in property (allowing for the few that may rent their principal residence and own homes elsewhere), a *fifth* are multiple property owners. Multiple property owners are disproportionately baby boomers, now aged between 52 and 71 years of age. These control half of all 'wealth held in additional properties' (Resolution Foundation, 2017). Because the Resolution Foundation analysis focused on *adults* rather than *households*, its assessment of wealth concentration in housing is rather more pronounced than the picture drawn above:

> Combined with falling home ownership since the early 2000s, the rise of second home-owning in 21st Century Britain has underpinned the increasing concentration of property wealth within a declining proportion of families. In contrast to the one in ten adults with multiple sources of property wealth, four in ten (40 per cent) adults have no property wealth at all, up from 35 per cent in 2000–02 and the same level as in 1993–95.
> (Resolution Foundation, 2017)

This account of wealth concentration is concerned with households normally resident in the UK and not owners based overseas. The point, however, is that property wealth is concentrated and has become more concentrated since the millennium. Because of housing's importance in wealth 'creation' (through the extraction of rent), this pattern of ownership and control has implications for future prosperity. Prosperity for the many can be achieved through the distribution of the resource itself or the income it generates. Redistributing the latter by either collecting rent through a progressive property tax or through a capital gains tax on sale (when rent is capitalised) will alter the balance of costs and benefits of ownership, causing a release of property onto the market, a fall in price and a redistribution of resource. The theory here is that land rent benefits will be spread in a more 'equal' way, through wider access to property ownership and through a democratisation of control over rent (through tax) which shifts more of that benefit to non-owners. In this way, overall patterns of consumption are flattened and a lower rate of growth is required to deliver the goal of shared and sustainable prosperity. Sayer captures much of this in his view that economics is fundamentally about 'provisioning': 'how societies provide themselves with the wherewithal to live' (Sayer, 2015: 20). Provisioning requires work, some of which is *directly* concerned with provisioning, while some has a more 'indirect relation to the production and distribution of goods and services' (p. 42). Whether direct or indirect, provisioning through work generates earned income for the worker, which is distinct from the unearned income derived, for example, from market exchange of a resource. Emerging from this discussion is the case to shift the tax burden away from provisioning through work, onto unearned income that is asset-based. There is a need to go back to the 'infancy of modern taxation' when it 'seemed obvious that the first thing that should be taxed was unearned income from rent' (p. 51).

Whitehead (2016: 419) has pointed to the need, over a sustained period, to build far more homes in England than rates of projected household formation would suggest are necessary. Building more homes than people need to live in will help satiate the nation's appetite to consume and extract income from property. With even higher rates of building, it may be possible to start to reverse the recent decline in owner-occupation (by shifting the ratio between workplace earnings and house prices in those locations where they are most stretched). But is this the type of 'housing growth' (and resource use) needed to deliver prosperity? Is the argument here that housing growth should substitute for housing equality, which could be otherwise delivered through a new relationship between people and assets, reshaped by shifting tax liability – carving out a bigger communal resource from the current and future housing stock? I return to this question in the next chapter.

Whose housing crisis?

England's housing crisis is reflected in more than just rising rents and a declining rate of owner-occupation. Reports of falling prices in particular submarkets (for example, London prime) or locations (for example, seaside towns in June 2018 – see BBC News, 2018e) are presented, in some quarters, as evidence of the surface nature of housing stress. The causes are not structural and costs rise and fall with the seasons and the market cycle. But what I have tried to show in this and previous chapters is that locally and generally observed stresses do indeed have structural roots. The economic relationship with housing, reviewed in Chapter 3, is pervasive: building housing is a means of maximising the rent potential of land. It has long been recognised that 'The richest crop for any field / Is a crop of bricks for it to yield / The richest crop that it can grow / Is a crop of houses in a row' (quoted in Sheppard, 1971: 92[1]). Once that housing is built, owners benefit from imputed and real rent. Its capitalised form (transformed into debt) supports lucrative primary and secondary mortgage markets, which deliver interest for banks and dividends for investors. Housing has a central role in value extraction, and is therefore commoditised and coveted. This same role also sustains the crises of inequality, social cohesion (and the breakdown of the 'generational contract') and prosperity which have been briefly analysed in this chapter.

Governments have a clear interest in tightly defining housing stress – as 'only' affecting sections of the urban poor or generation rent. Their interest lies either in setting targets that can be addressed in a single parliament (and winning elections on the back of novel or seemingly realistic ideas) or defending a particular ideological predilection. Regarding ideology, one might imagine big differences between political parties. The Conservatives are clear that 'owning property is a human right and a fundamental British liberty' (Planning Advisory Service, 2015; quoting the UK Housing Minister's response to suggestions that second home ownership might be more tightly controlled) and have traditionally resisted anything more than light regulation of housing markets. Labour's position had been remarkably

---

[1] Sheppard attributes this to Dyos, H.J. (1961) *Victorian Suburb: A Study of the Growth of Camberwell*, Leicester University Press: Leicester, p. 87. However, the original source appears to be Tarbuck, E.L. (1875) *Handbook of House Property: A Popular and Practical Guide*, Lockwood & Co.: London, p. 161. The latter author seems to be referring to a popular contemporary rhyme.

similar until quite recently, with one of its former leaders taken to task on the issue of housing consumption and rights:

> In 2013, a rich British man and his wife bought their seventh house in London – a four-storey, £1.35 million Georgian townhouse – for their twenty-seven-year-old son, Nicky, whose computer games firm and football agency were being dissolved five years after their launch. This would be just another story of the rich buying up more property than they can use if it were not that Nicky's father was former Prime Minister Tony Blair.
> (Dorling, 2014b: 105)

Under Jeremy Corbyn, there has been a significant change in tone, and many 'old Labour' policies – including the option of restarting public housebuilding – have been brought back into play. However, many Labour politicians remain focused on specific constituencies, especially the disadvantaged urban households who are reputedly being displaced by regeneration projects in London. Schemes that involve new partnerships with private developers and target 'estate renewal' (which can involve the replacement of high-quality – sometimes modernist – public housing, built to good space standards, with a mix of reputedly poorer-quality social housing and private development) have proven particularly controversial. Labour party critics have focused on the economy of refurbishment versus the expense of new build, arguing that communities' needs would have been better served by the former – and inner-urban gentrification would have been avoided. However, the big picture here is the structural predilection towards maximising land rent. Developers are drawn to these projects for profit and find willing partners among London boroughs, which are seeking to replace lost public funding (post the 2008 GFC) with new private income streams. They are increasingly driven by a financial logic, which is inevitable given their broad duty to deliver a range of public services – all of which cost money. It is underlying structures that generate these surface outcomes and that are more broadly responsible for the three core challenges – inequality, a loss of social cohesion and declining prosperity – that I have touched upon here.

In answer to this book's titular question – 'whose housing crisis?' – the broadest answer is that there can be no winners from social collapse under the weight of resource depletion and rising inequality. Friedman (2005) has drawn attention to the 'moral consequences' of growth, predicated on hope (or a lack of hope) for the future, but the moral consequences of social inequality, here and now, would seem to be the greater challenge. Housing is centrally positioned in a system of tax and reward that favours assets over work. But it is ultimately work that generates the real value that is siphoned off through housing, leaving a rising proportion of households indebted and impoverished.

6

An exit strategy

It is evident to many people that England is in the midst of a sustained housing crisis. The rapid decline in homeownership and spiralling private rents suggest that the crisis, measured in extraordinary affordability ratios between housing costs and stagnating workplace earnings, is deepening. An increasingly large part of the population, including *generation rent*, is locked out of the market and will remain locked out for the foreseeable future. Even regular incomes derived from good jobs will never catch up with soaring house prices, and those jobs will not allow aspiring homebuyers to accumulate big enough deposits to purchase their own homes. Many politicians have presented this as a *crisis of homeownership* (and declining 'asset ownership' – widening the intergenerational gulf): people are languishing in inferior tenures, especially private renting from amateur landlords, and cannot get a foothold on the housing ladder. Those already on that ladder – baby boomers and *buy-to-let* investors among them – are thought to be doing well. For them, this is someone else's crisis. They can relax, sit back and watch the value of their property grow, often 'earning' more from their homes than from their day jobs. But the backcloth to this is rising inequality, weakening social cohesion and concentrated wealth that does not deliver broader prosperity.

The road to this housing crisis (which I have described as one of cost, affordability and social justice) has been long and tortuous: the failure of successive governments to provide a mix of housing options across the market and social sectors; an overreliance on market production and allocation; bank and finance reregulation stretching back to the 1960s alongside the free flow of credit into the housing sector (supported by the expansion of a secondary mortgage market); tenancy deregulation and the predictable growth of amateur landlordism (alongside the additional investment pressure this generated); the increasing reliance on housing to underpin consumer confidence and drive the post-industrial economy since the Second World War; the looming crisis in state and private pensions; the failure to distinguish between the housing we need and the property we want to invest in, compounded by a failure to regulate that investment (turning housing into the asset class of choice) and now by the inflow of footloose global capital into cities like London.

In this book I have brought together two critical framings of housing outcomes in the UK, concentrating on England and on a cost crisis that is most visible in London and the wider southeast region.

First, and following Rittel and Webber's classic 1973 account of *Dilemmas in a General Theory of Planning*, England's housing crisis has all the features of a *wicked problem*: the manifest outcome of an incredibly complex set of inputs and circumstances which will not be resolved through any single action. The real crisis is perhaps recent governments' determination to boil the problem down into the simple need to build more houses, thereafter providing aspiring owners with purchase support – *help to buy* and stamp duty cuts – designed to aid the flow of more money into bricks and mortar. In some places, additional housing needs to be built. There has to be a *new supply response* to a basic lack of housing for purchase or rent. But building new homes is just one part of a bigger puzzle. And once that puzzle is pieced together – a task that I have attempted in this book – it becomes apparent that this is not just about the difficulty that many households encounter when trying to access homes that meet their needs, but also about an economy hooked on wealth extraction from land and property, once illiquid but now mobilised through the various tools of financialisation.

Second, and borrowing from Harvey's 1978 (and 1985) notion of an 'urbanisation of capital', delivered through the evolving instruments of that financialisation, the housing crisis and its drivers need to be seen in a broader economic context. The emphasis on building more *assets* for ownership (and for the absorption of capital and the extraction of value) is as much about achieving economic goals – supporting the construction sector, delivering asset-based welfare, building consumer confidence, and sustaining the country's vital financial services sector, comprising banks, financial intermediaries and investors – as social ones. Moreover, social goals are not always clearly defined, or are subordinate to an economic focus which is expected to tackle society's ills by delivering growth. But the fruits of that growth are unevenly shared, between owners and renters and between the old and the young. Therefore, challenges around social equality, cohesion and prosperity persist, with housing implicated in all.

Given the incredibly complex set of inputs and circumstances that have produced housing outcomes, the largely exclusive supply focus is pragmatic, allowing politicians to scapegoat planners (and the entrenched regulation that is said to stand in the way of unfettered market function) and tee up relatively easy answers – building more homes and 'ineffective knee-jerk and populist help for first-time-buyers' (Barker, 2014: xi) – that sidestep the need to grasp the nettle of 'unpopular taxation changes' (Barker, 2014: xi). Powerful forces are arrayed behind the status quo: a construction industry that wishes to continue to operate in much the same way as it has done for decades, extracting huge profits from land development; banks and investors accustomed to steady interest and dividends from the debt others accrue on property purchase; homeowners, who have sometimes struggled to buy their homes and now need to stay ahead of rising prices; and elites, for whom land and housing are sources of both wealth and status.

Is the current crisis resolvable while there is such vested interest behind the commodification and financialisation of housing? I suggested in the last chapter that there *should* now be broad support behind the case for change, as there will ultimately be no winners from the housing resource famine – and attendant socioeconomic mess – now confronting a great many people in England and other parts of the world. The aim in this final chapter is to examine possible counteractions to the housing crisis: responses to the propositions set out in Chapter 4. Because this book has been primarily concerned with the asset and home functions of housing, two types of necessary adjustment are examined: those that provide more immediate relief, but do not alter the relationship between assets and homes; and those that renegotiate that relationship in a manageable way.

Of the seven adjustments proposed, the first four operate within the current system while the last three are concerned with rebalancing the economic and social functions of housing, by regulating the flow of capital into residential property, capturing and redistributing land rent, or separating the housing we need to live in from the property we wish to extract income from. The rationale behind this mix of shorter- and longer-term adjustments is that housing occupies centre stage in the economic life of the nation, and therefore sudden and dramatic change needs to be avoided in favour of careful adjustments that gradually alter the way land and housing is consumed.

The four broad areas of shorter-term adjustment, each with its own set of particular actions and triggers, are as follows: (1) *build more homes* by making adjustments to planning and regulatory frameworks that will affect the environment for the development industry and accelerate new supply; take steps to (2) *curb certain types of direct investment in housing*; (3) *restore the public sector's role in direct provision*, not only through local housing companies, but also via grant funding for a modern equivalent of council housing; and encourage (4) *new models of housing delivery* – both private and collective – and hence increase new supply through that route.

The three longer-term, and necessarily phased, changes are as follows: to make a combination of (5) *adjustments to the tax system*, impacting on the balance of costs and rewards from housing consumption (linking to (2) above); and (6) *credit rationing and promoting new patterns of lending*. This consideration of some of the possible fronts that could be opened up against the housing crisis is followed by a proposal that addresses directly the conflation of homes, which deliver against a basic *need*, with the asset (and investment function) of property. A *new approach to planning for housing* – proposal (7) – is outlined, which aims to prioritise the delivery of *family homes* over other forms of residential property, while retaining some space for openly tradeable assets and other types of housing consumption, for recreation or investment.

Interim actions

1. Build more homes – through adjustments to planning/regulation

England's planning system is not perfect. Many critics have pointed to its shortcomings: to its occasional preoccupation with short-term regulation over long-term vision. Planning in England is rooted in the reformist zeal of the late nineteenth century: in the work of pioneers like Ebenezer Howard, who were uninterested in the bureaucracy of land-use control, but very interested in demonstrating how homes and livelihoods could be brought together in liveable, healthy and appealing new neighbourhoods. Critics of planning today often argue that vision has given too much ground to bureaucracy; ambition has been eclipsed by regulation (Ellis and Henderson, 2016). Planners and the planning system have received a lot of bad press. They are often (dis)credited with low-quality housing outcomes – which are, nevertheless, products of more than just regulation. They are sometimes mired in controversies around estate renewal, locked into difficult and unpopular relationships with the development sector. This book has not been centrally concerned with planning; others have tackled the failures of the system, and of recent legislation, head on (see Bowie, 2017). In Chapter 4, however, I explored some of the reasons why the 'permissioning' of sites for housing is not matched by rising output. In many areas, it is political rather than planning decisions that affect the buildout of potential housing sites, though the public perception is generally that local planning and politics are one and the same.

In a recent study commissioned by the RTPI, de Magalhaes et al (2018) have explored how 'greater planning certainty would affect residential development'. That study began by noting government's claim, in its 2015 Productivity Plan, that land-use planning is responsible for 'increasing the cost and uncertainty of investment, hence reducing the efficient use of land and other resources' (HM Treasury, 2015: 45). Government's answer was to reduce the burden of planning: to fast-track more modest development proposals (pp. 45–6). The Housing and Planning Act 2016 subsequently introduced 'permission in principle' for certain brownfield sites specifically listed in local registers. The question posed to de Magalhaes and colleagues was whether, through an upscaling of this initiative, *less planning* might deliver *more housing*. Answers to this question were sought through interviews and workshops with landowners, developers, consultants, finance providers, government officials, local authority officers, professional bodies and lobby groups. Planning risk (the 'journey' risks encountered through the regulatory process and the 'destination' risk of not achieving a viable permission) was conceived as a discrete obstacle lying in the path of private enterprise. But the research found that developers encounter a mix of ground, planning and finance risks that are difficult to untangle. The broader context of development (land in private ownership, legal frameworks, complex finance rules, the vagaries of the market and so on) favours large companies, which are better able to absorb risk by taking forward many schemes, in different places, at the same time. The ones that succeed, and deliver profit, will pay for the ones that fail. Granting planning 'in principle' will not reduce the need for more detailed scrutiny later on, as the site specifics of schemes are negotiated. The landowners, developers and finance providers who participated in the study saw no merit in having less planning. But like the HBF (2017) – cited in Chapter 4 – they agreed that composite development risk falls disproportionately on smaller housing providers. Applying permission in principle to the sorts of sites they are likely to develop could have a positive impact on net housing supply, if coupled with investment in *more planning* to support smaller companies and community groups bringing forward housing schemes. More planning – that is, a better resourced planning service – to ensure the necessary coordination between utilities and public bodies, is needed to make sure that more of the bigger schemes get off the ground. If this happens, if there is greater public investment in planning, then the need to factor failure into private business models – and required profit margins – may reduce, leading to the possibility of more housing being built at reduced cost to households.

2. Curb direct investment

There are many forms of direct investment in housing: owner-occupiers are enjoying 'in kind the rent [they] would otherwise receive in cash' (Thatcher, 1960) and are therefore motivated, at least in part, by investment; second home buying, *buy to let* (driven by rental yield – the 'capture of land rent' – rather than a desire to provide homes to others) and just buy to invest (it is no longer clear that 'buy to leave' investors actually 'leave', or at least not for lengthy periods, so 'buy to invest' would seem the safer label) are all means of capturing land rent, through annual yields or when capitalised on sale. The level of investment in each type will range from modest to grotesque, with both domestic and foreign buyers implicated across all. The other form of housing investment is passive, buying and trading in debt-backed securities that provide banks with their income streams for lending. Some curbs on direct investment have already been implemented: increases in stamp duty on second homes and tax relief rule changes for *buy to let*. It is also the case that more general tax measures and the *new approach to planning*, which I detail below, can be expected to change the balance of costs and rewards available to investors and place some necessary barriers in the path of certain forms of housing consumption. However, a number of bodies have now proposed specific restrictions on particular types of investment buying. The Resolution Foundation (2018: 219) has mooted the idea of giving 'city and city-regional mayors the authority to limit residential property purchases in housing hotspots to those resident in the UK'. I argued at the beginning of this book that there are no 'foreign villains' behind the housing crisis. But it is also clear that directly invested global capital is moving across an uneven playing field: many overseas buyers park their money in London housing because they are restricted from doing so either at home or in other major urban centres closer to home. The Resolution Foundation notes that 'outside of the UK, national and regional governments have … used either (or sometimes both) higher property transaction taxes or targeted regulations to dis-incentivise overseas buyers' (Resolution Foundation, 2018: 160). Other proposals, set out below, take a broader approach to 'pure investment' and do not single out any particular form. But in the interim, *equalising* the costs and rewards of property investment – across global cities – would seem to be a sensible and logical move, ensuring that it is *as welcome* in London as any other city with a deepening housing crisis. Chapter 5 has provided the broader case for doing so, in response to rising inequality and weakening social cohesion. Related ideas on direct investment are covered in sections (5) and (6) below.

3. Restore the public sector's role in direct provision

Tunstall (2015), cited earlier in this book, builds a persuasive case for state involvement in housing. Although the tide appears to have turned against public housing in the UK (the rewards from private ownership are now widely regarded as unquestionable), she shows that better housing is provided for more people when local authorities are building and letting good-quality council homes, funded through general taxation. The Labour Party's 2017 general election manifesto included a commitment to build 'at least 100,000 council and housing association homes a year for genuinely affordable rent or sale' (Labour Party, 2017: 60). More specifically, the party pledged to 'remove restrictions that stop councils from building homes and begin the biggest council building programme for at least 30 years' (p. 63). The 'ban' on 'long-term council tenancies' would also be lifted and the *right to buy* suspended. Any future government led by Jeremy Corbyn clearly intends to unpick major components of the last 40 years' of Conservative housing policy. There are also some hints as to how this might be funded: through a National Transformation Fund, aimed at 'upgrading the economy', by creating a National Investment Bank, and through increased income and corporation tax. The word 'land' (and therefore the term 'land tax') is absent from the manifesto.

There has been some indirect local authority development activity in England. The Local Government Act 2003 permits authorities to set up companies to provide products or services for profit (Hackett, 2017: 12). Reforms to the Housing Revenue Account (HRA) instigated by the last Labour Government in 2009, allowing councils to recycle receipts from *right to buy* sales and other income sources into direct house building, met resistance from the Coalition Government that took power in 2010. The Conservatives were far more interested in supporting indirect local authority development, through arms-length companies, rather than promoting direct public spending from the HRA. Hence, the 2011 Localism Act, building on earlier legislation, gave councils 'general powers of competence to carry out 'commercial purpose' and establish companies' (Hackett, 2017: 14). Research has since shown that 44% of authorities in England had set up companies by the end of 2017 (Morphet and Clifford, 2017: 44), building a total of 528 new homes in the five years since 2012 (Barker, 2018).

Christophers (forthcoming 2019) offers a broader perspective on these developments. He points out that local authorities displayed little interest in setting up companies before 2010. It was not until 'devolved austerity' began to bite, and funding to authorities was cut, that they looked for new sources of income (in support of the delivery of public services). Access to debt finance via the Public Loans Works Board – at close to sovereign prices – gave these companies a distinct edge over commercial competitors. Austerity and cheap credit underpins a post-crisis financial logic among English local authorities, which has been criticised in some quarters (especially by those private operators that have been undercut by the arms-length companies): one perspective says that they have transformed into 'grubby property developers' (Christophers, 2019), but another that they are simply playing the cards they have been dealt.

It is possible that local housing companies will come to play a bigger part in housing delivery in the future, but any housing they provide for social rent is merely a byproduct of commercial activity. This is not the programme of direct council build, funded by a transformation of HRA rules, envisaged in the Labour Party's manifesto. While preferential access to debt finance means that authorities can engage in *build to sell*, and also commercial *build-to-rent* models, meeting a full spectrum of need will require a return to direct funding.

4. New models of housing delivery

England's reliance on *build-to-sell* homes, delivered at industrial scale by large housebuilders, was detailed in Chapter 4, where the general case for moving to a more 'mixed' model of production was also presented. While the Home Builders Federation rejects the 'much-peddled myth that there exists an upper limit to the number of homes that can be produced by the private house building sector' (HBF, 2017: 24), it argues that the land and finance barriers impeding the entry of smaller providers into the business of housebuilding need to be reduced. Its particular concern is with those companies delivering fewer than 100 units each year. But the same barriers confront community and self-builders. Land is expensive: it represents a large part of total development cost. And finance is mostly available to companies with a proven record of delivering profitable schemes, which can lever borrowing or are supported by institutional investors. They are past winners in the development business and are regularly backed to win again. Arguably, the planning system could do more to support small providers, including through 'permission in principle' (see section (1) above), and general moves to recommunalise housing and democratise control over land rent could create a very different context for smaller players by reducing development costs and easing market entry. Proposals for moving in this direction are set out below.

Recent research has focused on the potential of self-build to add to the available mix of housing in England, how this model might be facilitated by planning and finance, and what difference it could make to overall housing availability. The UK is an outlier in terms of its reliance on a few big private companies to deliver most of its housing and in terms of the very low level of individually commissioned or built homes (Hamiduddin, 2017). Proponents of an enlarged self-build sector point to the many advantages of directly involving consumers and communities in the production of housing. Besides a *systemic resilience in diversity* argument – connecting a diversity of providers to a diversity of development opportunities and needs – involvement in the building of homes can bring positive social benefit, developing homes and communities simultaneously (Hamiduddin and Gallent, 2016). However, barriers confronting other models (including community land trusts) also stand in the way of self-build: these relate to land, finance and technical support. The Self-Build and Custom Housebuilding Act 2015 requires local authorities to maintain a register of people or groups seeking land on which to build their own homes. They must then have regard to the level of local interest in self-build when drawing up development plans and formulating policies on housing, land disposal and regeneration. The ambition behind this legislation is that the contribution of individually commissioned or built homes to total housing output could double in the next decade – rising to 20% by 2030.

Supporting people to build their own homes is not, of itself, a solution to the housing crisis. But impediments to self-build, and some of its advantages, parallel the structural drivers of that crisis. Housing is relatively cheap to build. Just over a decade ago, a number of housebuilders responded to the then Deputy Prime Minister John Prescott's *Design for Manufacture* competition (ODPM, 2006: 289) by demonstrating that new homes could be built for £60,000. While covering labour and materials, this cost excluded land. It is land that makes housing expensive to build and purchase. This is true for all producers, but it is self-builders, communities and others seeking to provide more affordable housing, who are squeezed from the market because of land cost. This is why local authorities – through housing companies – and many housing associations have turned to speculative market development in support of their social objectives. Full value must be extracted from land in order to pay for development, and it is only through the commercial practice of speculation (or building for known paying clients) that survival is possible. One of the advantages of self-build is the introduction of variety into the built environment – positive 'place-making' effects (Hamiduddin and Daseking, 2014). One of the visible markers of the housing crisis is the monotony of much residential development. Standardised housing designs reduce costs and risks. Land – the underlying asset – is often so expensive that developers are competing on cost rather than the quality of the housing they produce. Bringing down the land cost, by reducing its appeal as a tradeable asset and a source of value extraction, must be the primary response to the housing crisis. This can be expected to markedly increase the viability of different models of housing delivery – including self-build and community-based models – and more generally address spiralling costs across the market.

Renegotiating the assets–homes relationship

5. Adjustments to the tax system

Council tax is a source of local authority revenue. Taxpayers in London currently contribute to the cost of the services provided by the borough they live in and by the Greater London Authority. It is also a proxy for a land value tax, although the valuations on which it is based are now very old and council tax's limited banding structure (from A to H) means that the most valuable property and land is grossly undertaxed. Barker (2014: 66–7) argues that council tax tries to do too much and ends up doing nothing very well. There is certainly a case for extending council tax bands, as suggested by Dorling (2014a: 51), but this would not address the criticism that this wayward tax conflates too many functions. Extension of bands in the interim could be followed by a separation of local service funding and property/land taxation over the longer term. A 'local income tax' has been proposed as a means of covering the service component, with council tax transformed into a progressive property tax, based on regular revaluations. Local income tax would need to be redistributed by the Treasury to authorities, breaking the link between where tax is raised and spent. A better approach might be a local service levy, designed to avoid a similar backlash to that provoked by the Community Charge (or 'poll tax') in the early 1990s.

The more difficult part of this reform would be the property tax based on land value. Whatever the case for taxing wealth, voters have traditionally viewed such tax as unfair, preferring to contribute to public revenues from their workplace income. One way around this problem is to restore the Schedule A tax abolished in 1963, which presented imputed rent as a component of gross income. Barker (2014: 68) outlines the immediate challenges: 'such major reform would ... have an effect on relative house prices. It might have to be undertaken gradually to avoid market disruption, losses by lenders and the spread of negative equity.' The costs and rewards linked to asset and homeownership would shift, with impacts rippling through the economic system. The reality here is that no reform that impacts on relative house prices – and that seeks to address the housing cost crisis – will leave the banking and linked financial sector untouched. The case, however, for taxing land and therefore land rent is very strong. Control of that rent, arising from ownership of land and the buildings on it, is at the heart of rising wealth and housing inequality. A means of more fairly redistributing that rent will address the three core challenges – around inequality, social and intergenerational cohesion and prosperity – highlighted in the last chapter. In the past, right-leaning governments have won the argument for *not* taxing land value and rent by promising that more people will, in the future, share in the private benefits of asset ownership. The promotion and expansion of homeownership convinced an electoral majority that a progressive property tax was a bad idea. The more recent concentration of housing wealth in fewer hands and the rapid decline in owner-occupation has weakened this argument, and there may now be a growing constituency of voters in favour of more radical tax reform.

There are, however, many practical difficulties with regular land and property taxes (see Ryan-Collins et al, 2017: 202) that target asset-based wealth, including the logistics of regular valuation and re-valuation. That re-valuation, however, already happens when a property is sold – the buyer (or the buyer's bank) will require a valuation survey. If a primary residence is sold then the vendor will incur no capital gains tax or other proxy land tax. No assessment of capital gains liability is required for that transaction. An alternative to this approach is to levy capital gains on *all* residential property (which amounts to a tax on capitalised land rent) or to transform stamp duty, paid upfront by buyers, into a land value tax, paid by vendors. Stamp duty in its current form could be abolished, removing this impediment to mobility within the housing market. It could then be reconstituted as an onward sale tax, reflecting the rise in value between purchase and disposal. The tax take would remain unchanged (who pays the tax would be switched, but it would still be paid *on transaction*, at the same price point in the market). Much higher rates of stamp duty could be levied on the value uplift of non-primary residences including second homes and *buy to lets*, substituting for the current function of capital gains tax.

Different forms of land value tax can also be used to de-incentivise land banking (if this practice really occurs – see Chapter 4), hence impacting positively on the build-out of permissioned housing sites (reducing lag and lapse rates). More broadly, however, it has a role in reshaping the crucial costs and benefits arising from investment in housing, shifting the priorities of banks and investors, and changing the costs associated with housing as an asset class. But two further issues arise from all of this. First, if housing is implicated in the inner workings of the national economy, how can big changes be made without driving that economy into recession? Moreover, how might the lending focus of banks be steered away from land and property? Second, interventions through tax are complicated – and their goals may not be immediately apparent. Given that there is now a popular focus on housing and wealth inequality – underpinned by the fall in homeownership and wealth concentration in assets – might it be preferable to implement a more direct 'housing-branded' response, which appears more explicitly concerned with the 'fair distribution' of housing resource, underpinned by related tax reform? These issues are briefly addressed in the next two sections.

6. Credit rationing and promoting new patterns of lending

The enthusiasm among banks to lend on land and property is a key driver of the housing cost crisis. Banks compete with each other to create debt that can then be sold and traded in the secondary mortgage market. House prices are sustained by this process. Creating debt is profitable; creating more debt is even more profitable (Wainwright, 2009). The relationship between the money created by banks and house prices was examined earlier in this book. Keen (2018) argues that allowing private debt to outpace earnings is 'no way to run an economy' and sustains the cycle of growth and collapse in house prices. Bank lending should be restricted to 'some multiple of a property's actual or imputed rental income, so the income-earning potential of a property is the basis of the lending allowed against it'. A 1:10 ratio would mean that a maximum mortgage of £200,000 could be made on a property with a per annum rental yield of £20,000. 'The main function of such a rule', Keen argues, 'would be to break the reinforcing cycle that has given us globally over-valued housing and over-indebted households'. Because of the web of economic linkages from originator mortgages, through the secondary mortgage market, to the whole financial sector, such restrictions would trigger both a house price crash and a deep recession. Keen argues that it would be necessary, therefore, to start with a higher lending ratio – perhaps 1:20 – and then slowly reduce it over a number of years, allowing economies to adjust to these new circumstances.

What would that economic adjustment look like and how would it happen? Ryan-Collins et al (2017) have shown that banks have transformed into lenders on land and property. Investment in other sectors has dwindled as the flow of money into housing has increased. If restrictions were placed on property lending by private banks, the whole sector – banks and financial intermediaries – would face an immediate crisis. In theory, investment could be redirected to the 'real economy' of manufacturing and production. But in practice, would a sector that has receded in recent years be in a position to suddenly absorb surplus capital and reverse its own decline? The groundwork for rebalancing the national economy needs to be led by the public sector in advance of restrictions on property lending or any other interventions – through tax or planning – that try to shrink capital investment in housing. Rebalancing the economy away from housing would require a new pattern of lending/investment that supports innovation and new business startups. In 2017, the Labour Party argued in its general election manifesto, that 'our financial system is still holding back too many of our small businesses and local economies' (Labour Party, 2017: 16). The proposed response was the creation of a 'National Investment Bank that will bring in private capital finance to deliver £250 billion of lending power' (p. 16). This bank, it was claimed, will:

> support a network of regional development banks that, unlike giant City of London firms, will be dedicated to supporting inclusive growth in their communities. The banks will deliver the finance that our small businesses, co-operatives and innovative projects need across the whole country. The National Investment Bank will fill existing gaps in lending by private banks, particularly to small businesses, and by providing patient, long-term finance to R&D-intensive investments. (Labour Party, 2017: 16)

Government needs to play a central role in rebalancing the national economy. City of London firms have been encouraged to change their lending strategies – including at the annual Mansion House dinners – but the unbroken trajectory over the last 40 years has been towards property-related lending. Ryan-Collins et al (2017: 211) point out that 'although land-backed collateral gives the appearance of security, in fact land-backed assets are inherently risky for banks since they are generally much more illiquid, with long maturities, than banks' liabilities'. It makes sense for banks to shift the balance of lending towards business loans – as holding land and property assets 'makes banks' balance sheets more pro-cyclical' (p. 211) (increasing the risk of being caught out in liquidity crises). But government needs to spearhead movement in this direction, supporting the first waves of growth in R&D and the business sector, thereby creating the conditions for capital switch back to the primary circuit.

7. A new approach to planning

Again, the planning system, and its potential to engineer different housing outcomes, has not been a primary focus of this book. The instruments of land-use control, including legal agreements and conditions, are regularly used to deliver affordable housing or restrict the occupancy of new-build homes to buyers or purchasers with specific characteristics. This happens when permission for development is granted: that permission often requires a condition being met and an agreement to that end is reached with the developer. It can mean, for example, the inclusion of a minimum proportion or number of 'affordable units', or a requirement that homes are only occupied by people living or working full-time in a defined area. Legally binding agreements and conditions are used to alter market outcomes. This is possible because development rights were nationalised after the Second World War and the state, represented by local planning authorities, has bounded discretion – within the framework of adopted local plans – to grant or deny the right to develop land for defined uses. Public interventions, through the planning system, are grounded in evidence that ordinary market processes would not meet the complexities of local need (and instead deliver housing that would be unaffordable to many people on local wages). They are badged as essential disruptions that seek compromise with landowners and development actors. A proportion of the cost of providing non-market homes or of reserving homes for local need is captured from the development process and retained by local authorities or third-sector partners.

This arrangement is necessary in England because land is in private ownership. Ways must be found to capture some of that value for necessary public investments and infrastructure. Elsewhere, having a high proportion of land under public ownership – for example, in Singapore, Hong Kong and South Korea – means that governments can invest upfront in infrastructure on their own land, prepare that land for development and then sell leases to private developers, hence recovering costs and generating public revenues. The Lyons Housing Review (2014) has suggested bringing some land into public ownership for housing use, revising existing laws on *compulsory purchase* (eminent domain) and compensation so that land can be acquired at close to existing rather than intended use value (which prevents effective *value capture* by the local state). Building social housing on that land would ensure that either rents remain affordable in perpetuity or onward sale prices could be regulated. If housing for private sale were built, it would need to be on fixed-term lease to ensure that value can be retrieved at a later date. A progressive property tax could also ensure the retention of an element of land rent.

The reality in England is that land is not, for the most part, in public ownership and there is little prospect of imminent nationalisation. The planning system has, however, demonstrated its potential to engineer compromises with the market. Some of these have been mainstreamed and include negotiating contributions of affordable units. Others remain more peripheral and are applied only in particular contexts. In rural areas, for example, the purchase of second homes has been occasionally addressed through the use of general occupancy conditions – stipulating that new-build homes must be occupied by agricultural workers or, more recently, on a 'full-time basis' (see Satsangi et al, 2010: 141–52). Because these are locally applied, they tend to affect geographical patterns of development activity: housebuilders shift their business to areas where there is no restriction. And because conditions affect only the new-build segment (being set when schemes are permissioned), they can cause a transfer of investment demand to the second-hand market and push local house prices onto an elevated upward track (Shucksmith, 1990: 127). One of the challenges of planning intervention in the market is that it is piecemeal, tied to local evidence and particular circumstances. At a systemic level, emphasis is placed on defending private property rights and the capacity of local markets to find their own price points, and thereafter serve the needs of local populations. This seldom happens, and piecemeal intervention – corrections through planning that lead to a wider array of needs being addressed – is required.

I have noted previously that a number of commentators have laid the blame for the housing crisis at the planning system's door, contending that local regulators have stood in the way of necessary housing being built. I agree that the system could play a bigger part in ensuring that England has the housing it needs. But this will not happen through neoliberal actions: deregulation or the relaxing of land-use rules, or through a disempowering of local authorities in favour of permitted development or permission in principle (see earlier discussion in this chapter). It could, however, be achieved by upscaling the sorts of interventions noted above: by tasking planning authorities to allocate land for the housing that is needed before allocating for openly tradeable property of the type desired by investors. An entirely new approach to planning could be devised that defends not *the human right to own property* (in any quantity) but *the universal right to a secure and stable home*. Occupancy conditions try to achieve this in a local and limited way, but encounter the difficulties noted above. Reflections on the limitations of occupancy conditions occasionally turn to the potential of engineering a dual property market through the Use Classes Order (UCO), a secondary instrument which lists those material changes of land use that require planning permission (last reviewed 6 April 2018). In relation to second homes, it is frequently argued that the UCO could be used to distinguish between 'dwelling houses' occupied on a full-time or on a seasonal basis (see Gallent et al, 2005: 168). Regulation currently makes no such distinction and a dwelling house remains a dwelling house 'whether or not [it is] a main residence'. Subcategories (a, b and c) indicate whether a house is occupied by a single person or family, by up to six people receiving care or by some other group of up to six occupants – perhaps a religious community. The proposal to create a 'second home' subcategory – C3(d) today – was made by nationalists in Wales in the 1980s and by a Labour MP in the 1990s, only to be described by the Conservatives as 'spiteful and impractical' (Gallent et al, 2005: 168). The question now is whether the declining level of owner-occupation and hardships in the private rental sector are enough to win broader support for creating a dual housing market through planning and whether this could be reconciled with housing's wider economic function.

Planning could be used to distinguish between *resident/family* and *investment* housing, with local plans primarily or exclusively allocating land to meet the objectively assessed need for resident/ family homes (with that use class, now C3a, covering the three current subcategories of C3, deleting the 'whether or not a main residence' clause). There could then be an extension from this point beyond land-use planning into related purchase restrictions and tax rules. The aim with 'resident/family dwelling houses' would be to bring down cost, relative to local earnings, in perpetuity, and therefore prevent the accumulation of capitalised land rent (realised on sale, making them potentially unaffordable to successive buyers). That could be achieved, for example, by charging capital gains tax on these properties (at a rate designed to impact substantially on future price inflation, but allowing householder improvements to be set against the liability). The combination of planning and tax rules suggested here would recast the function of most new housing – as homes for living in rather than vessels for wealth extraction. Investors might, however, try to take advantage of their lower onward sale price and attempt to capture land rent though *buy to let*; to prevent that, 'single families' or 'single people' would be restricted to owning just one resident/family house. Inevitably, the value of land allocated for this revised C3a use would be generally depressed: whether or not land would be sold and developed would depend on the value of land for alternative, non-housing uses. There would inevitably be resistance to such intervention and perhaps subdued private sector interest. That would leave an opportunity for *local housing companies* (see earlier discussion) to bring these sites forward, assembling land under new compulsory purchase and compensation rules if necessary. Also, the depression of land values would be less than that caused by current occupancy restrictions, which set very tight limits on who can rent or buy housing. Resident/family housing rules would allow anyone needing to live and/or work in an area to buy or 'trade up' to one of these homes. The market for such housing is potentially huge and includes the third of private renters (roughly two million households) who aspire to buy their own homes but for whom ownership has been thus far out of reach.

This particular exit strategy tries to deal with three pressures and drivers: first, the aspiration of many people to own the homes they live in; second, the accumulation and concentration of wealth in housing, which is causing housing costs to outpace workplace earnings; and third, the desire – in many quarters – to maintain an open segment of the market in which housing can be bought and traded for profit (but with that profit reasonably taxed). I can see no reason why the development industry would not adapt to such a system once embedded. The ambition to consume housing as luxury and for status competition, displaced from this controlled market, would find an outlet in other parts of the market, but would no longer prevent younger households – or those without accumulated property wealth – from buying their own homes. The price of resident/family housing would, because of limits on trading and the prevention of consumption for investment, find a new lower ceiling. But in that segment of the market that remained open, increased scarcity – leading to potentially higher land and property prices – will mean the retention of investment interest, and therefore the retention of tax contribution from 'prime property'.

There are benefits and likely pitfalls from this strategy. Tax on resident / family housing would need to be calibrated to support some equity growth (in a market in which homes are sought after and being actively traded), providing families with the means to meet transaction and moving costs and therefore enabling them to relocate when they need to. Other use classes could be established to support additional housing models, such as rented homes delivered by community land trusts, or these might be permitted within the resident/family class. The current system presents a hostile environment to community and mutual housing models, mainly because of the high price of land, but these could be supported within a framework of greater planning control. Self-build could be expected to flourish in this dual housing market. One of the potential pitfalls, however, is that the appetite for higher capital returns from property investment would result in surging demand for second-hand property and climbing prices in that segment. This issue would need to be dealt with through progressive taxation and classification of existing property according to the new schema. An owner of multiple homes might, for instance, need to register one (their current primary residence) as a resident/family home, with associated tax rules and trading restrictions, retaining others as investment housing. The national stock of family/resident homes would therefore match the current number of owner-occupied primary residences and the vast majority of new additions to that stock would be in the same class. Over time, the balance of types would shift (because of the priority given to resident/family homes in land allocations and in new development) but a stock of investment property would be retained, increasing its value and relative tax contribution. Extensions to this approach could include the selective reclassification of *buy to let* properties as resident/family homes, but with owners granted a period of time in which to sell properties to resident buyers, perhaps encouraged to do so through a tax amnesty. Irrespective of the detail, the goal of this market disruption would be to more broadly and equitably share the benefits of home-ownership by curtailing investment in the *owner-occupied* sector.

An exit strategy

Ways need to be found to reduce the concentration of wealth in housing, by shifting the balance of costs and rewards for housing consumption. It has taken close to 150 pages of review, commentary and analysis to reach two possible formulae for shifting housing outcomes and inequalities in England: either *those with property wealth should contribute more through taxation and those without should contribute less*; or steps should be taken to *engineer a dual housing market, splitting resident/family from investment housing*. Tax reform would need to be staged, so as to reduce the economic shock. The objective would be to ensure that property and unearned income figures more prominently in tax calculations, with the tax burden transferred from work to assets, from income onto wealth extraction. For working households, this could mean the payment of tax on imputed rent as a component of income tax (back to Schedule A). For non-working households – those not taxed Pay As You Earn or without regular workplace earnings – the new liability might be collected once rent is capitalised on sale, when a household moves or following disposal of estate. The objective of this first formula is to change the relative value of work and assets: to ensure that *work pays* and there is reduced reliance on housing as a support for personal finance and national economies. The second formula – the related alternative of engineering a dual housing market – would establish a new binary between homes and assets. It would also aim to reduce reliance on housing as an investment asset within the controlled market but preserve an open market for investment. The goal of retaining an open segment would be to cushion the economy from the effects of sudden market closure and leave space for other housing models, including *build to rent*. But the primary intent would be to ensure that housing is available and accessible for those aspiring to *purchase* and live in their own homes. It recognises that *ownership* – and the in-kind rent it delivers – is important to households through the lifecycle and, if extended in a fair way, would help lessen critical inequalities. Implementing such a system, however, would present challenges; but if the development industry were slow to embrace this new reality, local housing companies might step in to develop homes on allocated land. Keen's proposed credit rationing – supported by a number of other commentators – offers another exit route. But, like the tax and planning formulae set out above, it would need to be accompanied by serious and concerted efforts to wean banks off property-related lending.

The full complexity of how such big shifts would work, and the impacts they would have, are beyond the scope of a single book. Fortunately, there are now many contributions to this debate, some with a focus on land and housing and others with a broader perspective on growth, prosperity and inequality. It is easy to reject these general principles, and the strategies set out above. Powerful interests are arrayed against them, because they cannot be reconciled with established property rights, 'fundamental British liberties', or the expectation that housing should perform as any other asset, delivering equity growth that, for some owners, far exceeds workplace earnings. Housing is a *wealth machine* that works well for a few but not for the many. The choice before us, in the face a deepening housing crisis, is between an unimaginable level of housebuilding – in response to unbounded market demands on housing and derivative debt products – and what is, to many people, an unthinkable reorientation of our housing, planning and tax systems.

Many households in England endure very serious housing stress: a situation in which 'one part of the population is pitted against the other, with those who own gaining directly from the rising prices that exclude everyone else' (Minton, 2017: 30). Access to homes is restricted by a range of cost drivers and pressures, with housing regularly turned into pure asset in support of a broader economic transformation. The housing question remains an economic question, and the crisis a condition of late capitalism, with nations pursuing unequal and unsustainable growth over shared prosperity. It is also a crisis of social justice: a broken contract in which the *right to housing* has been abandoned. It is that right that needs to be reclaimed.

References

Aalbers, M. (2015) The Great Moderation, the Great Excess and the global housing crisis, in *International Journal of Housing Policy*, 15, 1, pp. 43–60

Aalbers, M. (2016) *The Financialization of Housing: A Political Economy Approach*, London: Routledge

Adams, D. (2011) The 'wicked problem' of planning for housing development, in *Housing Studies*, 26, 6, pp. 951–60

Andrew, M., Evans, A., Koundouri, P. and Meen, G. (2003) *Residential stamp duty: Time for a change*, accessed 5 July 2018 at: https://mpra.ub.uni-muenchen.de/38264/1/MPRA_paper_38264.pdf

Armstrong, A. (2016) Commentary: UK Housing Market: Problems and Policies, in *National Institute Economic Review*, 235, 1, pp. F4–8

Arrighi, G. (1994) *The Long Twentieth Century: Money, Power, and the Origins of Our Times*, London and New York: Verso

Atkinson, R., Burrows, R. and Rhodes, D. (2016a) Capital city? London's housing markets and the 'super-rich', in Hay, I. and Beaverstock, J. V. (Eds) *Handbook on Wealth and the Super-Rich*, London: Edward Elgar, pp. 225–43

Atkinson, R., Burrows, R., Glucksberg, L., Ho, H-K., Knowles, C., Rhodes, D. and Webber, R. (2016b) *International Capital Flows into London Property: SPERI Global Political Economy Brief No. 2*, Sheffield: SPERI

Atkinson, R., Parker, S. and Burrows, R. (2017) Elite formation, power and space in contemporary London, in *Theory, Culture and Society*, 34, pp. 179–200

Bank of England (2018) *Lending to Industries – Headline Flows*: data on this topic accessed July 2018 at: https://www.bankofengland.co.uk/statistics/visual-summaries/businesses-finance-raised

Barker, K. (2004) *Review of Housing Supply*, London: HM Treasury

Barker, K. (2006) *Review of Land Use Planning: Final Report – Recommendations*, London: HMSO

Barker, K. (2014) *Housing: Where's the Plan?*, London: London Publishing Partnership

Barker, N. (2018) Councils set up 58 housing companies since 2012, in *Inside Housing*, 16 February 2018, accessed 29 June 2018 at: https://www.insidehousing.co.uk/news/news/councils-set-up-58-housing-companies-since-2012-54634

BBC News (2004) Why your parents are ripping you off, 23 March 2004, accessed 22 June 2018 at: http://news.bbc.co.uk/1/hi/programmes/if/3520800.stm

BBC News (2016) Councils spent £3.5 billion on temporary housing in the last 5 years, 17 November 2016, accessed 23 November 2018 at: https://www.bbc.co.uk/news/uk-38016728

BBC News (2018a) Theresa May: Young are 'right to be angry' about lack of homes, 5 March 2018, accessed 8 March 2018 at: www.bbc.co.uk/news/uk-politics-43279177

BBC News (2018b) Russian spy: What now for the Russia/UK relationship, accessed 8 March 2018 at: www.bbc.co.uk/news/uk-43318103

BBC News (2018c) Thousands join TUC march over wages and workers' rights, 12 May 2018, accessed 17 May 2018 at www.bbc.co.uk/news/business-44093870

BBC News (2018d) Tax on pensioners proposed to heal intergenerational divide, 8 May 2018, accessed 22 June 2018 at https://www.bbc.co.uk/news/business-44029808

BBC News (2018e) House prices tumble in seaside hotspots, 22 June 2018, accessed 26 June 2018 at https://www.bbc.co.uk/news/business-44575400

Beauregard, R. A. (1994) Capital switching and the built environment: United States, 1970–89, in *Environment and Planning A*, 26, pp. 715–32

Benson, M. and Hamiduddin, I. (Eds) (2017) *Self-build Homes: Social Discourse, Experiences and Directions*, London: UCL Press

Bentley, D. (2016) *Housing Supply and Household Growth, National and Local: Briefing Note*, London: Civitas

Bowie, D. (2017) *Radical Solutions to the Housing Supply Crisis*, Bristol: Policy Press

Bramley, G. (1993) Land-use planning and the housing market in Britain: The impact on housebuilding and house prices, in *Environment and Planning A*, 25, 7, pp. 1021–51

Bramley, G. and Leishman, C. (2005) A local housing market model with spatial interaction and land-use planning controls, in *Environment and Planning A*, 37, pp. 1637–49

Bramley, G. and Watkins, D. (2016) Housebuilding, demographic change and affordability as outcomes of local planning decisions: Exploring interactions using a sub-regional model of housing markets in England, in *Progress in Planning*, 104, pp. 1–35

British Property Federation (2017) *Unlocking the Benefits and Potential of Build to Rent*, London: BPF

Cheshire, P. (2009) *Urban Containment, Housing Affordability and Price Stability: Irreconcilable Goals*, London: Spatial Economics Research Centre (SERC), LSE

Cheshire, P. (2014) Turning houses into gold: The failure of British planning, accessed 5 July 2018 at: http://blogs.lse.ac.uk/politicsandpolicy/turning-houses-into-gold-the-failure-of-british-planning

Cheshire, P., Nathan, M. and Overman, H. G. (2014) *Urban Economics and Urban Policy: Challenging Conventional Policy Wisdom*, London: Edward Elgar

Christophers, B. (2010) On voodoo economics: Theorising relations of property, value and contemporary capitalism, in *Transactions of the Institute of British Geographers New Series*, 35, pp. 94–108

Christophers, B. (forthcoming 2019) Putting financialisation in its financial context: transformations in local government-led urban development in post-financial crisis England, unpublished – forthcoming

Churchman, C. West (1967) Guest editorial: Wicked problems, in *Management Science*, 14, 4, pp. B141–2

Civitas (2014) *Finding Shelter: Overseas Investment in the UK Housing Market*, accessed 21 September 2017 at: www.civitas.org.uk/publications/finding-shelter/

Clarke, G. (2012) DCLG Press Release, accessed 22 November 2018 at https://www.gov.uk /government/news/planning-reforms-will-deliver-local-growth-with-community-support--2

Coelho, M., Dellepiane-Avellaneda, S. and Ratnoo, V. (2017) The political economy of housing in England, in *New Political Economy*, 22, 1, pp. 31–60

Cole, I. (2012) Housing market renewal and demolition in England in the 2000s: The governance of 'wicked problems', in *International Journal of Housing Policy*, 12, 3, pp. 347–66

Cole, I. and Furbey, R. (1994) *The Eclipse of Council Housing*, London: Routledge

Council of Mortgage Lenders (2016) Still small but growing: How have landlord characteristics changed since 2010?, 8 August 2016, accessed 26 June 2018 at: https://www.cml.org.uk/news/news-and-views/still-small-but-growing-how-have-landlord-characteristics

Crook, T., Whitehead, C. and Henneberry, J. (2016) *Planning Gain: Providing Infrastructure and Affordable Housing*, London: Wiley

Daly, H. E. (1997) *Beyond Growth: The Economics of Sustainable Development*, Boston, MA: Beacon Press

De Magalhaes, C., Freire-Trigo, S., Gallent, N., Scanlon, K. and Whitehead, C. (2018) *Planning Risk and Development: How Greater Planning Certainty Would Affect Residential Development*, London: RTPI

Department of the Environment (1980) Land for private house-building, Circular 9/80, London: HMSO

Department of the Environment (1984) Land for housing, Circular 15/84, London: HMSO

Dianati, K., Zimmermann, N. and Davies, M. (2017) London's Housing Crisis, Paper presented at the 35th Annual Conference of the System Dynamics Society, 16–20 July, Cambridge, MA

Dolphin, T. and Griffith, M. (2011) *Forever Blowing Bubbles? Housing's Role in the UK Economy*, London: IPPR

Dorey, P. (2011) *British Conservatism: The Politics and Philosophy of Inequality*, London and New York: Palgrave Macmillan

Dorling, D. (2014a) *All That is Solid: How the Great Housing Disaster Defines our Times, and What we can do about it*, Harmondsworth: Penguin

Dorling, D. (2014b) *Inequality and the 1%*, London: Verso

Dorling, D. (2015) Policy, politics, health and housing in the UK, in *Policy & Politics*, 43, 2, pp. 163–80

Duca, J. V., Muellbauer, J. and Murphy, A. (2010) Housing markets and the financial crisis of 2007–2009: Lessons for the future, in *Journal of Financial Stability*, 6, 4, pp. 203–17

Edwards, M. (2002) Wealth creation and poverty creation, in *City*, 6, 1, pp. 25–42

Edwards, M. (2015) *Prospect for Land, Rent and Housing in UK Cities*, London: Government Office for Science

Ellis, H. and Henderson, K. (2016) *English Planning in Crisis: 10 Steps to a Sustainable Future*, Bristol: Policy Press

Engels, F. (1872 [1970]) *The Housing Question*, Moscow: Progress Publishers

Evans, A. W. (1991) 'Rabbit Hutches on Postage Stamps': Planning, Development and Political Economy, in *Urban Studies*, 28, 6, pp. 853–70

Evening Standard (2017) 'Tens of thousands' of people living in beds in sheds across the capital, report says, 20 December 2017, accessed 15 June 2018 at: https://www.standard.co.uk/news/politics/tens-of-thousands-of-people-living-in-beds-in-sheds-across-the-capital-report-shows-a3723786.html

Fagleman, D. (2015) *Devo Home: A Double Devolution of Housing to People and Places*, London: ResPublica

Fernandez, R. and Aalbers, M. B. (2016) Financialisation and housing: Between globalization and varieties of capitalism, in *Competition and Change*, 20, 2, pp. 71–88

Fernandez, R., Hofman, A. and Aalbers, M. (2016) London and New York as a safe deposit box for the transnational wealth elite, in *Environment and Planning A*, 48, pp. 2443–61

Field, M. and Layard, A. (2017) Locating community-led housing within neighbourhood plans as a response to England's housing needs, in *Public Money and Management*, 37, 2, pp. 105–12

Friedman, B. M. (2005) *The Moral Consequences of Economic Growth*, New York: Random House

Gallent, N. (2005) Regional housing figures in England: Policy, politics and ownership, in *Housing Studies*, 20, pp. 973–88

Gallent, N. (2016) Investment, global capital and other drivers of England's housing crisis, in *Journal of Urban Regeneration and Renewal*, 9, 2, pp. 122–38

Gallent, N. (2018) Planning for Housing – The Global Challenges Confronting Local Practice, in Ferm, J. and Tomaney, J. (Eds) *Planning Practice: Critical Perspectives from the UK*, Routledge: London, pp. 205–19

Gallent, N., Durrant, D. and May, N. (2017) Housing supply, investment demand and money creation: A comment on the drivers of London's housing crisis, in *Urban Studies*, 54, 10, pp. 2204–16

Gallent, N., Durrant, D. and Stirling, P. (2018) Between the unimaginable and the unthinkable: pathways to and from England's housing crisis, in *Town Planning Review*, 89, 2, pp. 125–44

Gallent, N., Tewdwr-Jones, N. and Mace, A. (2005) *Second Homes: European Perspectives and UK Policies*, Aldershot: Ashgate

Gamble, A. (2014) *Crisis without End? The Unravelling of Western Prosperity*, London: Palgrave

Gotham, K. F. (2006) The secondary circuit of capital reconsidered: Globalisation and the US real estate sector, in *American Journal of Sociology*, 112, 1, pp. 231–75

Gotham, K. F. (2009) Creating liquidity out of spatial fixity: The secondary circuit of capital and the subprime mortgage crisis, in *International Journal of Urban and Regional Research*, 33, 2, pp. 355–71

The Guardian (2015a) Generation rent: How does it feel to be locked out of the housing market? 23 July 2015, accessed 4 July 2018 at: https://www.theguardian.com/uk-news/2015/jul/23/generation-rent-locked-out-of-housing-market

The Guardian (2015b) London council in 'social cleansing' row over bid to move tenants to Birmingham, 6 May 2015, accessed 4 July 2018 at: https://www.theguardian.com/society/2015/may/06/london-council-social-cleansing-row-move-tenants-to-birmingham

The Guardian (2015c) George Osborne tears up planning laws so Londoners can add storeys to homes, 9 July 2015, accessed 24 November 2018 at: https://www.theguardian.com/politics/2015/jul/09/osborne-tears-up-planning-laws-londoners-build-extra-storeys-on-homes

Gurran, N. (2018) Global home-sharing, local communities and the Airbnb debate: A planning research agenda, in *Planning Theory and Practice*, 19, 2, pp. 298–304

Gurran, N., Gallent, N. and Chiu, R. (2016) *Politics, Planning and Housing Supply in Australia, England and Hong Kong*, London: Routledge

Hackett, P. (2017) *Delivering the Renaissance in Council-built Homes: The Rise of Local Housing Companies*, London: Smith Institute

Hall, P. (2001) Sustainable cities or town cramming? In Batty, S., Layard, A. and Davoudi, S. (Eds) *Planning for a Sustainable Future*, London: Routledge, pp. 101–14

Hall, P., Thomas, R., Gracey, H. and Drewett, R. (1973) *The Containment of Urban England*, London: Allen and Unwin

Halligan, L. (2018) Home truths: Part IV: How ministers made the housing crisis worse, 17 April 2018, accessed 12 November 2018 at: https://unherd.com/2018/04/home-truths-part-iv-ministers-made-housing-crisis-worse

Hamiduddin, I. (2017) Creating high quality places through community-led housing, Scottish Urban Regeneration Forum, accessed 29 June 2018 at: https://www.surf.scot/scotregen/creating-high-quality-places-through-community-led-housing

Hamiduddin, I. and Daseking, W. (2014) Community-based planning in Freiburg, Germany: the case of Vauban, in Gallent, N. and Ciaffi, D. (eds) *Community Action and Planning: Contexts, Drivers and Outcomes*, Bristol: Policy Press, pp. 237–59

Hamiduddin, I. and Gallent, N. (2016) Self-build communities: the rationale and experiences of group-build (*Baugruppen*) housing development in Germany, in *Housing Studies*, 31, 4, pp. 365–83

Harvey, D. (1978) The urban process under capitalism: A framework for analysis, in *International Journal of Urban and Regional Research*, 2, 1–3, pp. 101–31

Harvey, D. (1985) *The Urbanization of Capital*, Baltimore, MD: Johns Hopkins University Press

Harvey, D. (1989) *The Condition of Postmodernity*, Oxford: Blackwell

Hilber, C. (2015) *UK Housing and Planning Policies: The Evidence from Economic Research*, London: LSE

Hilber, C. and Schöni, O. (2018) The economic impacts of constraining second home investments, Centre for Economic Performance Discussion Paper 1556, London: London School of Economics

Hilber, C. and Vermeulen, W. (2010) *The Impacts of Restricting Housing Supply on House Prices and Affordability: Final Report*, London: DCLG

HM Treasury (2015) *Fixing the Foundations: Creating a More Prosperous Nation*, London: TSO

Holmans, A. E. (2014) *Housing Need and Effective Demand in England: A Look at 'the Big Picture'*, Cambridge: Cambridge Centre for Housing and Planning Research

Home Builders Federation (2014) *Barker Review: A Decade On*, London: HBF

Home Builders Federation (2017) *Reversing the Decline of Small Housebuilders: Reinvigorating Entrepreneurialism and Building More Homes*, London: HBF, accessed 8 June 2018 at: https://www.hbf.co.uk/documents/6879/HBF_SME_Report_2017_Web.pdf

Housebuilder (2017) Britain's top 25 housebuilders, accessed 7 June 2018 at https://www.house-builder.co.uk/news/britains-top-25-housebuilders

Hulchanski, J. D. (1995) The concept of housing affordability: Six contemporary uses of the housing expenditure-to-income ratio, in *Housing Studies*, 10, 4, pp. 471–91

Jackson, T. (2009) *Prosperity without Growth: Economics for a Finite Planet*, London: Routledge

Jones, C. and Murie, A. (2006) *Right to Buy: Analysis and Evaluation of a Housing Policy*, London: Blackwell

Keen, S. (2017) *Can We Avoid Another Financial Crisis?* Cambridge: Polity Press

Keen, S. (2018) The housing crisis: there's nothing we can do… or is there? EcoCognito Blog, accessed 14 June 2018 at: www.ecocognito.com/twitawoo/post/housing-crisis-explained-nothing-we-can-do

Kotlikoff, L. J. and Burns, S. (2005) *The Coming Generational Storm. What You Need to Know about America's Economic Future*, Cambridge, MA: MIT Press

Krippner, G. R. (2005) The financialization of the American economy, in *Socio-economic Review*, 3, 2, pp. 173–208

Labour Party (2017) *For the Many, Not the Few: The Labour Party Manifesto 2017*, London: Labour Party

Lichfields (2017) *Stock and Flow: Planning Permissions and Housing Output*, London: Nathaniel Lichfield and Partners

Logan, J. R. and Molotch, H. L. (2010) The city as a growth machine, in Brown-Saracino, J. (Ed) *The Gentrification Debates*, New York: Routledge, pp. 87–102

Lyons, M. (2014) *The Lyons Housing Review: Mobilising Across the Nation to Build the Homes Our Children Need*, accessed 10 November 2016 at: www.yourbritain.org.uk/uploads/editor/files/The_Lyons_Housing_Review_2.pdf

Mace, A., Blanc, F., Gordon, I. and Scanlon, K. (2016) *A 21st Century Metropolitan Greenbelt*, London: London School of Economics

Machin, S. (2015) Real Wage Trends, conference paper presented at Understanding the Great Recession: From Micro to Macro Conference, Bank of England, 23 September 2015, accessed 29 November 2015 at: https://www.ifs.org.uk/uploads/Presentations/Understanding%20the%20recession_230915/SMachin.pdf

Maclennan, D. and Miao, J. (2017) Housing and capital in the 21st century, in *Housing, Theory and Society*, 34, 2, pp. 127–45

Meen, G. (2011) A long-run model of housing affordability, in *Housing Studies*, 26, 7–8, pp. 1081–1103

Milne, A. and Wood, J. A. (2014) An old fashioned banking crisis: credit growth and loan losses in the UK 1997–2012, in Chadha, J. S., Chrystal, A., Pearlman, J., Smith, P. and Wright, S. (Eds) *The UK Economy in the Long Expansion and its Aftermath*, Cambridge: Cambridge University Press, pp. 210–43

Ministry of Housing, Communities and Local Government (2018a) *English Housing Survey: Headline Report 2016–17*, London: MHCLG

Ministry of Housing, Communities and Local Government (2018b) *National Planning Policy Framework: Draft Text for Consultation*, MHCLG: London

Minton, A. (2017) *Big Capital: Who is London For?* London: Penguin Random House

Moore, T. and McKee, K. (2012) Empowering local communities? An international review of community land trusts, in *Housing Studies*, 27, 2, pp. 280–82

Morphet, J. and Clifford, B. (2017) *Local Authority Direct Provision of Housing*, London: National Planning Forum and Royal Town Planning Institute

Motesharrei, S., Rivas, J. and Kalnay, E. (2014) Human and nature dynamics (HANDY): Modelling inequality and use of resources in the collapse or sustainability of societies, in *Ecological Economics*, 101, pp. 90–102

Muellbauer, J. (2005) Property taxation and the economy after the Barker Review, in *The Economic Journal*, 115, 502, pp. 99–117

Muellbauer, J. and Murphy, A. (2008) Housing markets and the economy: The assessment, in *Oxford Review of Economic Policy*, 24, pp. 1–33

Murie, A. (2016) *The Right to Buy? Selling off Public and Social Housing*, Bristol: Policy Press

Nathan, M. and Overman, H. G. (2011) *What We Know (and Don't Know) About the Links between Planning and Economic Performance*, SERC Policy Paper 10, London: SERC

National Planning and Housing Advice Unit (2007) *Meeting the Housing Needs of an Aspiring and Growing Nation*, London: DCLG

New Economics Foundation (2016) Why you can't afford a home in the UK, 16 February 2016, accessed 12 November 2018 at: https://medium.com/@neweconomics/why-you-can-t-afford-a-home-in-the-uk-44347750646a

ODPM (2006) *Affordability and the Supply of Housing: Session 2005–06*, London: TSO

OECD (2011) *Perspectives on Global Development 2012: Social Cohesion in a Shifting World*, Paris: OECD Publishing

OECD (2017) *Revenue Statistics 2017: The United Kingdom*, Paris: OECD Centre for Tax Policy and Administration

Office for Budget Responsibility (2011) *Fiscal Sustainability Report, July 2011*, London: OBR

Office for Budget Responsibility (2012) *Council Tax Receipts*, London: OBR

Office for Budget Responsibility (2016) *Forecast Evaluation Report, October 2016*, London: OBR

Office for Budget Responsibility (2018) *Tax by Tax, Spend by Spend*: data on this topic accessed July 2018 at: https://obr.uk/forecasts-in-depth/tax-by-tax-spend-by-spend/

ONS (2016) UK House Price Index: September 2016, Figure 2: Average UK house price, January 2005 to September 2016, accessed 27 November 2018 at: https://www.ons.gov.uk/economy/inflationandpriceindices/bulletins/housepriceindex/sept2016

ONS (2018a) House price to workplace-based earning ratio, London: ONS, accessed 22 November 2018 at: https://www.ons.gov.uk/people populationandcommunity/housing/datasets/ratioofhouseprice toworkplacebasedearningslowerquartileandmedian

ONS (2018b) Gross Domestic Product: data on this topic accessed July 2018 at: https://www.ons.gov.uk/economy/grossdomesticproductgdp

ONS (2018c) Index of Services: data on this topic accessed July 2018 at: https://www.ons.gov.uk/economy/economicoutputand productivity/output/bulletins/indexofservices/february2018

ONS (2018d) Index of Production: data on this topic accessed July 2018 at: https://www.ons.gov.uk/economy/economicoutputand productivity/output/bulletins/indexofproduction/march2018

Osborne, G. (2014) Mansion House 2014: Speech by the Chancellor of the Exchequer, London: HM Treasury. Accessed 22 November 2018 at: https://www.gov.uk/government/speeches/mansion-house-2014-speech-by-the-chancellor-of-the-exchequer

Pahl, R. (1975) *Whose City? And Further Essays on Urban Society*, Harmondsworth: Penguin

Paris, C. (2010) *Affluence, Mobility and Second Home Ownership*, London: Routledge

Pawson, H., Hulse, K. and Morris, A. (2017) Interpreting the rise of long-term private renting in a liberal welfare regime context, in *Housing Studies*, 32, pp. 1062–84

Piketty, T. (2014) *Capital in the Twenty-First Century*, Cambridge, MA: Harvard University Press

Planning Advisory Service (2015) Advice from Planning Advisory Service in regard to second homes, accessed 26 June 2018 at: https://www.dorsetforyou.gov.uk/media/207891/Planning-Advisory-Service-advice-on-second-homes/pdf/Second_Homes_Advice.pdf

Resolution Foundation (2017) 21st Century Britain has seen a 30 per cent increase in second home ownership, 19 August 2017, accessed 26 June 2018 at: https://www.resolutionfoundation.org/media/press-releases/21st-century-britain-has-seen-a-30-per-cent-increase-in-second-home-ownership

Resolution Foundation (2018) *A New Generational Contract: The Final Report of the Intergenerational Commission*, London: Resolution Foundation

Rhodes, C. (2016) *Historic Data on Industries in the UK: Briefing Paper 06623*, London: House of Commons Library

Rittel, H. W. and Webber, M. M. (1973) Dilemmas in a general theory of planning, in *Policy Sciences*, 4, 2, pp. 155–69

Rolnik, R. (2013) Late neoliberalism: The financialization of homeownership and housing rights, in *International Journal of Urban and Regional Research*, 37, pp. 1058–66

Rossall Valentine, D. (2015) *Solving the UK Housing Crisis*, London: The Bow Group

Rossi, U. (2017) *Cities in Global Capitalism*, Cambridge: Polity Press

RTPI (2007) *Opening up the Debate: Exploring Housing Land Supply Myths*, London: Royal Town Planning Institute.

Ryan-Collins, J., Greenham, T., Werner, R. and Jackson, A. (2012) *Where Does Money Come From? A Guide to the UK Monetary and Banking System*, London: Positive Money

Ryan-Collins, J., Lloyd, T. and MacFarlane, L. (2017) *Rethinking the Economics of Land and Housing*, London: Zed Books

Sassen, S. (2014) *Expulsions: Brutality and Complexity in the Global Economy*, Cambridge, MA: Harvard University Press

Satsangi, M., Gallent, N. and Bevan, M. (2010) *The Rural Housing Question: Communities and Planning in the British Countryside*, Bristol: Policy Press

Saunders, P. (1978) Domestic property and social class, in *International Journal of Urban and Regional Research*, 2, 1–3, pp. 233–51

Saunders, P. (1984) Beyond housing classes: The sociological significance of private property rights in means of consumption, in *International Journal of Urban and Regional Research*, 8, 2, pp. 202–27

Sayer, A. (2015) *Why We Can't Afford the Rich*, Bristol: Policy Press

Scanlon, K., Whitehead, C. and Blanc, F. (2017a) *The Role of Overseas Investors in the London New-build Residential Market*, London: London School of Economics

Scanlon, K., Whitehead, C. and Blanc, F. (2017b) *A Taxing Question: Is Stamp Duty Land Tax Suffocating the English Housing Market*, London: London School of Economics

Schwartz, H. and Seabrooke, L. (2008) Varieties of residential capitalism in the international political economy: Old welfare states and the new politics of housing, in *Comparative European Politics*, 6, 3, pp. 237–61

Sheppard, F. (1971) *History of London: London 1808–1870: The Infernal Wen*, Berkeley, CA: University of California Press

Shucksmith, M. (1990) *Housebuilding in Britain's Countryside*, London: Routledge

Soaita, A. M. (2018) *Mapping the Literature on Housing Taxation in the UK and other OECD Countries*, Glasgow: UK Collaborative Centre for Housing Evidence

Stephens, M. (2007) Mortgage market deregulation and its consequences, in *Housing Studies*, 22, 2, pp. 201–20

Stirling, P. (2019) National Housing Strategy and Market Mediation in London, unpublished PhD thesis (forthcoming), London: University College London

Thatcher, M. (1960) Do you qualify for a refund? In *Finchley Press*, 18 March 1960, accessed 17 May 2018 at: https://www.margaretthatcher.org/document/101063

Tummers, L. (2016) The re-emergence of self-managed co-housing in Europe: A critical review of co-housing research, in *Urban Studies*, 53, 10, pp. 2023–40

Tunstall, B. (2015) Relative housing space inequality in England and Wales, and its recent rapid resurgence, in *International Journal of Housing Policy*, 15, pp. 105–26

Urban Task Force (1998) *Towards an Urban Renaissance: Final Report of the Urban Task Force Chaired by Lord Rogers of Riverside*, London: DETR

Verity, J. (2018) Firms on Caribbean island chain own 23,000 UK properties, BBC, 13 February 2018, accessed 5 July 2018 at: www.bbc.co.uk/news/business-42666274

Wainwright, T. (2009) Laying the foundations for a crisis: Mapping the historico-geographical construction of Residential Mortgage Backed Securitization in the UK, in *International Journal of Urban and Regional Research*, 33, 2, pp. 372–88

Wallace, A., Rhodes, D. J. and Webber, R. (2017) *Overseas Investors in London's New Build Housing Market*, London: Greater London Authority

Watson, M. (2010) House price Keynesianism and the contradictions of the modern investor subject, in *Housing Studies*, 25, 3, pp. 413–26

Wetzstein, S. (2017) The global urban housing affordability crisis, in *Urban Studies*, 54, 14, pp. 3159–77

Whitehead, C. M. E. (2016) Using projections of household numbers: Tensions between planning and economics, in *Town and Country Planning*, 85, 10, pp. 415–21

Whitehead, C. M. E (2017) Stamp Duty Land Tax is suffocating the housing market, LSE News, 11 November 2017, accessed 8 June 2018 at: www.lse.ac.uk/News/Latest-news-from-LSE/2017/11-November-2017/Stamp-Duty-Land-Tax-is-suffocating-the-housing-market

Whitehead, C. M. E, Sagor, E., Edge, A. and Walker, B. (2015) *Understanding the Local Impact of New Residential Development: a Pilot Study*, London: London School of Economics

Wilkinson, R. and Pickett, K. (2010) *The Spirit Level: Why Equality is Better for Everyone*, London: Penguin Books

Index

Page numbers in *italic* refer to a figure in the text.

Lightning Source UK Ltd.
Milton Keynes UK
UKHW020635100522
402764UK00007B/795